Problem Solving:
A Cognitive Approach

Hank Kahney

Open University Press
Milton Keynes · Philadelphia

Open University Press
12 Cofferidge Close
Stony Stratford
Milton Keynes MK11 1BY, England
and
1900 Frost Road, Suite 101
Bristol, PA 19007, USA

First published 1986
Reprinted 1989
Copyright © The Open University, 1986

British Library Cataloguing in Publication Data

Kahney, Hank
  Problem solving : a cognitive approach.
  (Open guides to psychology)
  1. Problem solving
  I. Title   II. Series
  153.4'3   BF441

ISBN 0–335–15327–5

Library of Congress Cataloging in Publication Data

Kahney, Hank.
  Problem solving.
  (Open guides to psychology)
  Bibliography: p.
  Includes indexes.
  1. Problem solving.   2. Cognition.   I. Title
  II. Series.
  BF441.K24 1986   153.4'3   85–21651

ISBN 0–335–15327–5 (pbk.)

Typeset by Mathematical Composition Setters Ltd, Salisbury, UK.
Printed and bound in Great Britain at the Alden Press, Oxford

*This book is dedicated to the memory
of my little brother Kenny, 1941–1980*

Problem Solving: A Cognitive Approach

Contents

Part III Representation and Acquisition of Cognitive Skills

Preface

Within the Open Guides to Psychology series *Problem Solving: A Cognitive Approach* is one of a companion set of four books, the others being *Language Understanding, Memory*, and *Perception and Representation*. Together these form the main texts of the Open University third level course in Cognitive Psychology, but each of the four volumes can be read on its own. The course is designed for second or third year students. It is presented in the style and format that the Open University has found to be uniquely effective in making the material intelligible and interesting.

The books provide an up-to-date in-depth treatment of the major issues, theories and findings in cognitive psychology. They are designed to introduce a representative selection of different research methods, and the reader is encouraged, by means of Activities and Self-assessment Questions interpolated through the text, to become involved in cognitive psychology as an active participant.

The author gratefully acknowledges the many helpful comments and suggestions of fellow members of the course team on earlier drafts. He would also like to thank Ken Kotovsky, Matthew Lewis, Peter Pirolli and Jeff Shrager for their many helpful comments on parts of this book.

Introduction

This book is divided into three parts. Part I discusses early research on problem solving by cognitive psychologists. The aim is to introduce you to some of the tools that were developed during this period for carrying out problem-solving research. Part I also introduces one of the main themes of the book, which concerns the effects of experience in learning and problem solving. Part I also presents a very influential theory of human problem solving, devised by H. A. Simon, which depicts man as an active processor of information. Parts II and III discuss modifications or elaborations of Simon's information processing model, exploring the role and limits of cognitive representations and processes in learning to solve problems.

In Part II we turn again to questions about the role of previous experience in problem solving. Here we will consider some of the mechanisms that psychologists have suggested are involved in identifying and utilizing past experience in solving new problems. A computer model of these processes is described.

Part III considers recent research on problem solving by novices and experts in various domains of knowledge, and computer implementations of the types of processes involved in problem solving.

There are, however, topics of major interest to psychologists interested in thinking and learning that are not covered in this book. The major omissions are studies of rational and irrational reasoning processes. There is a huge literature on the topic of logical reasoning, and I recommend the following books as good introductions to this area of research. First, there is Richard E. Mayer's text on problem solving called *Thinking, Problem Solving, Cognition*, published by W. H. Freeman, 1983. This text not only discusses research on deductive and inductive reasoning, but also provides a very good coverage of the historical roots of the cognitive approach to problem solving. There is a long section devoted to considering the applications and implications of the cognitive approach. A second recommended text is John R. Anderson's *Cognitive Psychology and its Implications*, published by W. H. Freeman, 1980. This book is more of a standard undergraduate psychology textbook, and gives good coverage of perception, memory and language as well as problem solving.

How to use this guide

Throughout this book you will find a number of Self-assessment Questions (SAQs) and Activities. These have been designed to help you become an active participant in understanding and applying the concepts presented in the text. Attempting all of the SAQs will help you to assess what you have and have not understood in the preceding sections, and will also provide you with an opportunity to organize what you have learned. The Activities often present you with an opportunity to experience for yourself the kind of difficulties experimental subjects have when they tackle particular problems, and the problems confronting a psychologist who wants to understand what is going on when people solve some kind of problem. You will find the answers to the SAQs at the end of the book.

The book also contains a number of Techniques Boxes which describe various experimental techniques that have been used by psychologists in studying learning and problem solving. Each main section in the book ends with a Summary which highlights the main points that have been made. There is an Index of Concepts at the end of the book which indicates the page on which a concept is first introduced and defined.

Part I
Introduction to Problem Solving

Part I   Introduction to Problem Solving

Contents

1   *Introduction*

Here is a list of problems. Some of them you will recognize as familiar, reflecting the concerns of most people in our culture, while others will be problems with which you are unconcerned yourself, but that you would recognize as problems for certain other people. Some of the problems you may never have heard of, even though they are probably the simplest of all the problems in the list. If you haven't heard of them, they're the ones problem-solving researchers have studied in psychological laboratories.

How do you write the Great American Novel?
How am I going to pay this bill?
What's the best way to avoid tomorrow's predicted traffic jam?
How am I going to pass this examination?
How do I beat this guy at Nim?
What does 'anaphoric' mean?
Where's that Philips's screwdriver?
How can I get out of that appointment on Thursday so I can go to see the Rolling Stones?
How can I divide the water in the first jug between that jug and a second jug using only the three jugs provided?
How can you draw four straight lines through a three-by-three array of nine dots without taking your pen off the paper?
How can I avoid person X?
How can I attract person Y?
How can I motivate my children to make the most of their schooling?
Starting with three rings on one peg, how can I move all the rings to a third peg without breaking the rules?

All of the above problems have two things in common. First, they all specify a *goal*, whether it is paying a bill or knowing the meaning of an unfamiliar word. Secondly, in each case the solver is not immediately able to achieve the goal. These facts can be used as a basis for a definition of the concepts of *problem* and *problem solving*. Whenever you have a goal which is blocked for any reason – lack of resources, lack of information, and so on – you have a problem. Whatever you do in order to achieve your goal is problem solving.

Perhaps the most important aim of problem-solving research is the development of a theory of problem solving that explains the interactions between problem situations and the people who are confronted by the problem. To paraphrase Greeno (1978), we would like to be able to say, 'Look, there are essentially five (or ten or fifteen or whatever) types of problem. Any problem you name can be categorized as one of these types, or some combination of them.' If we were able to categorize problem types we could devote our research efforts to understanding the strategies used by people who are successful at solving particular categories of problems. Once we knew that, we could revolutionize educational practice by teaching students successful strategies for solving all kinds of problems. That's the dream. But the development of a general theory of problem solving is a complex undertaking. Even the very small list of problems at the beginning of this Introduction indicates that the range of problems is vast. It would be difficult, too, for most people to say what any two of these problems have in common.

One of the dominating questions in problem-solving research concerns the effects of experience on subsequent problem-solving efforts. The first time we are confronted with a particular problem we may experience difficulties in solving it. But when we are faced with the same problem again and again, or with a series of similar problems, we expect to get better and better as we benefit from our experience. Improved performance as a result of solving a number of similar problems is a phenomenon called *positive transfer*. Sometimes, though, the effects of experience can result in *negative transfer*. This occurs when previous experience interferes with the solution to a current problem.

For example, if England changed the colour of green traffic lights to blue, we could expect people to learn to 'go' at blue lights fairly quickly (positive transfer of our knowledge of green lights). But imagine the consequences of reversing the colours; red to go and green to stop. Your old knowledge would definitely (and perhaps fatally) interfere (negative transfer).

Transfer effects have been studied by presenting a subject with problems which may appear different in their surface characteristics but which have the same or a very similar underlying structure. However, it is not sufficient merely to claim that problems that 'look different on the surface' are 'really the same underneath'. What is required is some rigorous method for revealing the underlying structure of problems, and making comparisons between these basic structures. One goal of Part I is to introduce you to a technique for defining the structures of problems − called '*state space analysis*' − and to show how it has been used to investigate questions about transfer of learning.

Given that we could categorize the structures of problems, the next question we need to consider concerns the processes and strategies adopted by problem solvers. One research method involves studying a single type of problem in depth. One such problem type is known as a *transformation problem* (Greeno, 1978), because it involves moves which transform one situation into another. Various transformation problems will be introduced later, but you can get an intuitive feel for the type of problem by considering the task of mixing paints. If you want a light shade of grey, and you have some black paint and some white paint, you could pour a bit of white paint into the black and mix the paints together, that is, transform the state of the black paint by mixing it with white. The result is the shade of grey you want to end up with or it is still the wrong shade. If it is correct, you stop. If not, you pour in some more white paint and mix again (second transformation). So transformation problems can be defined as problems that require 'moves' which transform one state (black) into another state (grey). Most of Part I of this book is devoted to a discussion of research on such problems, primarily because a great amount of research effort has been devoted to problems of this general type. Indeed, Simon (1978) points out that most of what we know about learning and problem solving was discovered by analysing the behaviour of people solving transformation problems.

Equally important, the problems are simple and interesting enough for you to do a considerable amount of research on your own, partly for the fun of it and partly for the experience of studying problem-solving processes at first hand.

Summary of Section 1

- A person has a 'problem' when he or she has a goal which cannot be achieved directly.
- Any action taken by a person in pursuit of a blocked goal, whether physical or mental, is regarded as problem solving.
- A major goal of problem-solving research is the development of a theory of problem solving which will make it possible to categorize the structures of problems and investigate successful problem-solving strategies.
- Transfer of learning involves understanding how material learned at one point in time affects the learning of other material. Experience with earlier tasks may either facilitate (positive transfer) or hinder (negative transfer) the solving of related material.
- Some of the best researched problems in psychology belong to a class called transformation problems, which involve 'moves' that transform one state into another. The analysis of people's behaviour in solving such problems has laid the foundation for understanding problem solving in more complex situations.

17

2   *Getting started on problem solving*

Activity 1 contains an example of a typical transformation problem – the *Towers of Hanoi problem*. Solving the problem involves moves which transform one state of the problem into another state. In Activity 1 the problem is presented in the way it is normally given. But there are also instructions on how to set up the problem using coins and paper for your own attempt at the problem.

Activity 1
What I would like you to do is get out a tape recorder and 'think out loud' while you are solving the problem. Try to say everything you think about while you work on the problem. So, as you work on the problem you will be deciding what moves you should make. You will also have a reason for making the moves. You should describe both out loud and record them. You will be able to transcribe the tape (make a record of its contents) at a later time. If you don't have access to a recorder, make a written record of the decisions you take in solving the problem and your reasons for them. This record is called a *protocol*.

The Towers of Hanoi   Starting with three rings of different sizes – a small (SSS) ring, a medium-sized (MMM) ring, and a large (LLLLLLL) ring – on Peg A (see 'Initial situation' below), your task is to move all of the rings to Peg B (as in the 'Goal situation') in the shortest number of moves. Your solution is subject to the following constraints: (1) you can only move one ring at a time, and (2) you may not place any ring on top of a smaller ring. (And, of course, rings may only be placed on one of the three pegs, not placed on, for example, the table or floor.)

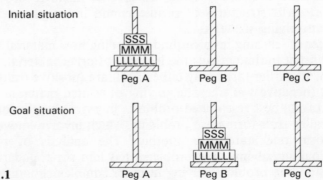

Figure 1.1

In order to set up this problem, get out a piece of paper and draw three circles side by side, about two inches apart, and, starting from the circle on the left, label them 'Peg A', 'Peg B' and 'Peg C' respectively. Then place three different sized coins on 'Peg A', with the largest on the bottom and the smallest on the top. Finally, moving the coins one at a time and without ever placing a coin on top of a smaller one, transfer all the coins over to 'Peg B'.

SAQ 1
What is the minimum number of steps needed to solve the three-ring Towers of Hanoi problem? How many steps (moves) did you take in solving the problem?

You might find it incredible that researchers think they can learn anything about real-world problem solving by creating 'toy worlds' – puzzle-like tasks such as the Towers of Hanoi problem. However, there is nothing intrinsically wrong with studying simple, even contrived, phenomena. This is like engineers making small models for use in wind tunnels. All sciences create 'toy worlds' for close examination, mainly because the real world is very complex and messy. As psychologists we are interested in what we learn from studying toy worlds only to the extent that it helps us to understand how people behave in the real world, which is the actual focus of our interest.

Researchers have spoken of numerous advantages in using simple tasks in laboratory studies of problem solving. One advantage is that no prior special knowledge is necessary. People are given all the information they need in order to solve problems such as the Towers of Hanoi, so investigators do not have to worry about different people bringing different amounts of knowledge to the task. Another advantage is that the same problem can be dressed up in different guises and researchers can use this fact to ask questions about the effect of experience with one problem when a subject is confronted with a new problem having the same underlying structure. Still another advantage is that whole families of problems can be developed from one of the core problems. For example, the Towers of Hanoi problem can be made more difficult simply by adding to the number of rings that have to be moved from one peg to another.

Finally, as Simon (1978) pointed out, real-world problems often take hours, days, perhaps even a working lifetime to solve (without any guarantee of success). On the other hand, even complex versions of the Towers of Hanoi problem (and others) can be solved by most people, usually in an hour or less. Because such relatively short solution times are involved, experimenters are able to shift attention from the question of whether or not a person succeeds in solving a problem to the question of *how* he or she solves it.

In the 'real world', transformation problems occur in domains such as logic, physics and mathematics as well as in mixing paints and cocktails. If studies of toy-world problems really are pertinent to real-world concerns, then what we learn about problem solving in the simpler situations should help us to understand problem solving in the more complex situations. And indeed cognitive psychologists have begun to test their ideas in the classrooms of high schools and colleges. (We will take up this strand of the story in Part III.)

2.1   Well-defined and ill-defined problems

One distinction often made between real-world problems and laboratory problems is how well they are defined. In a *well-defined problem*, that is, in a well-structured problem, the solver is provided with all the information needed in order to solve the problem. In well-defined problems the solver is provided with four different sorts of information:

1 information about the *initial state* of the problem;
2 information about the *goal state;*
3 information about legal *operators* (things you are allowed to do in solving the problem);
4 information about *operator restrictions* which constrain the application of operators.

We can illustrate the notion of a well-defined problem with reference to the Towers of Hanoi problem. Look back to the instructions in Activity 1 and re-read the problem statement. The information given is the following:

1 *Initial state.* In the Towers of Hanoi problem the initial state is the set of three different-sized rings piled up in a particular way on peg A, an empty peg, Peg B, to the right of Peg A, and another empty peg, Peg C, on the extreme right.
2 *Goal state.* The goal state is achieved when the set of different-sized rings are piled up on Peg B, with the small ring on top, the large ring on the bottom, and the medium-sized ring in the middle of the pile.
3 *Operators.* Only one operator is explicitly mentioned in the problem statement – the 'move' operator. The operator allows the solver to move rings from one peg to another.
4 *Operator restrictions.* There are three restrictions placed on the use of the 'move' operator:
(a) the solver is allowed to move only one ring at a time;

(b) the solver is not allowed to place a larger ring on top of a smaller ring;

(c) the solver is not allowed to place rings anywhere except on one of the three pegs.

SAQ 2
Fill in the initial states and goals for:
(a) Solving a crossword puzzle clue.

   Initial state:

   Goal state:

(b) Playing noughts and crosses.

   Initial state:

   Goal state:

An *ill-defined problem*, that is, an ill-structured problem, is one in which little or no information is provided on the initial state, the goal state, the operators, or some combination of these. An example of an ill-defined problem is how to pass an examination in psychology. If you try to analyse such a problem in terms of initial and goal states, operators and operator restrictions, you'll see that the task is only vaguely defined. The initial state includes a list of examination questions, information about the number of questions you are required to answer, and the total amount of time allowed for the examination. In broad terms the goal state is 'getting the grade you want'. If you want a grade A, your answers will have to be better than the answers you might give if you would be happy just to pass the examination. But how would you know whether you've provided answers that will gain a pass, or an A? That is, how can you tell when the goal has been achieved?

The operators that can be brought to bear – none of which are made explicit on the examination paper – are things like retrieval of information from memory (what did the lecturer say?), making notes of information, organizing information, deleting unusable information, planning an answer, writing, editing, and so forth. Some operators that might normally be used, such as asking another student what he or she thinks, or looking in books and notes, are explicitly forbidden, and restrictions on operators such as writing have time constraints, so decisions have to be made about how to divide time between organizing and writing answers to each question.

In short, in ill-defined problems the solver has to define the problem for himself. This point draws our attention to the fact that degree of structure comes down to a question of a solver's own knowledge. For instance, consider your experience with the Towers of Hanoi problem. The particular problem you solved was the 'three ring' problem, but any number of rings might be involved. Suppose I now said, 'Can you do the Hanoi problem for me again? We'll use five rings this time. I want you to transfer them to Peg C'. The problem will now seem pretty well defined to you even though a lot of information about the initial state, goal state, operators and restrictions on operators has not been provided. Someone who had never heard of the Towers of Hanoi problem would find the above statement of the problem very ill defined.

This is because you are able to augment the problem *givens* (the information provided at the beginning of a problem is often referred to as the problem givens, or 'given' information) with knowledge retrieved from long-term memory. When people have had enough experience with a particular type of problem they internalize the structure of those problems, and as a consequence are able to treat as well structured problems that seem ill structured to anyone who has little or no experience with such problems. When a solver's knowledge is taken into account, the boundary between ill- and well-defined problems becomes somewhat blurred. In fact, most problems should be treated as having more or less definition, or structure, than others, rather than as belonging in one category or the other. For example, Greeno (1976) has pointed out that there are many problems that are quite well defined even though problem solvers treat them in such ways that they have 'indefinite' goals. Greeno draws his examples from problem solving in geometry, in which students are often set the goal of, say, proving two triangles congruent. There are a number of ways in which such a goal can be achieved, and the solver need not have a specific set of goal features in mind at the start of the problem in order to recognize a solution when one has been achieved. Greeno argues that that is all a person needs in order to solve such problems – the ability to recognize a solution when it arises. In solving such problems solvers work forward, gathering information that will be useful in achieving the goal.

In terms of everyday problems, imagine setting out to do your shopping for the weekend. The goal is to get in enough food to feed the family for three days. This goal is pretty indefinite in that you don't have any specific meals in mind. When you get to the butcher's shop you consider the meats on display as you wait your turn to be served. There's liver – but the kids don't like it. Everybody likes steak, so that's a possibility – but not at those prices. What about that turkey? They all like turkey; you haven't prepared a turkey for a long time; you have all the other ingredients you need; the leftovers can be used to make a curry (another meal). This is a clear example of information gathering during the process of solving a problem, and fitting it in with the problem givens – family likes and dislikes, how much time you are prepared to spend on preparing meals, what other ingredients you already have that would make a particular meal possible, and so on.

Another example would be 'getting away from it all'. You could pack the kids and your spouse into the car and just head out into the country with the indefinite goal of 'having a good time'. You might see a place that would be nice for a picnic. (And, of course, you might *not* see a place that would be nice for a picnic, in which case the idea of having a picnic would perhaps not occur to you.) Or you might discover a village that would be nice for sightseeing. In short, possible solutions arise while you are working on the problem of having a nice day out, and, because you know the things you like doing, you are able to recognize situations that satisfy your goal. As Greeno points out, the addition of problems with indefinite goals to the category of problems described as well defined considerably broadens the boundaries of well-defined problems.

SAQ 3
Would you consider the problem of getting from London to Paris a well-defined problem or an ill-defined problem? Why?

Summary of Section 2

- Researchers construct 'toy worlds' like the Towers of Hanoi problem in which to study problem-solving processes because the short solution times and lack of prior knowledge allow them to study people's problem-solving strategies.
- One way of classifying problems is in terms of the degree to which they can be described as well defined or ill defined.
- Well-defined problems are those for which the initial state, goal state, and legal operators and operator restrictions are all given at the start of the problem.
- An ill-defined problem is one in which information about either the initial or goal state, or the operators, is incomplete and has to be supplied by the problem solver.

3   *State space analysis*

In this section we will discuss an important tool for problem-solving research called *state space analysis*. This particular tool is important first of all in providing a representation of the underlying structure of problems. We will see that two problems can seem quite different 'on the surface' but that they in fact have the same underlying problem structure – and that as a result they also have the same solution. Interestingly, when people are given problems having identical underlying structures but different 'cover stories', they often fail to detect the close relationship between the problems. In this case, knowing the solution to one problem does not make the solution to the second problem easier. Moreover, even when people are told that such a relationship exists, they often fail to benefit from the solution of one of the problems in their attempt at solving the other.

3.1   *Analysing problem structures*

State space analysis involves constructing a diagram containing complete information about everything a solver could do, using only the rules of the problem. In order to demonstrate this notion, consider Figure 1.2 which shows the initial state (or state 1) of the Towers of Hanoi problem which you were asked to solve in Activity 1.

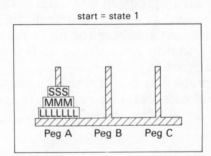

Figure 1.2

Given the rules of the game (only one ring can be moved at a time, and no ring can be placed on top of a smaller one) there are two possible 'legal' moves from state 1: move the small ring from Peg A to either Peg B or Peg C. Figure 1.3 shows the problem states that would result from making either of these two moves, that is, state 2

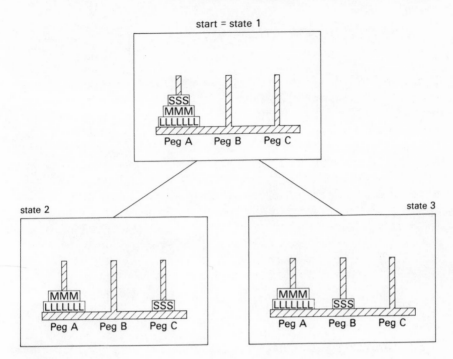

Figure 1.3

or state 3. The lines linking state 1 with state 2 and state 1 with state 3 stand for the application of the move operators (i.e. 'move small ring from Peg A to Peg B' and so forth) which transform one state of the problem into another state.

At state 2 of the problem, three moves are possible under the rules. First, the small ring could be moved back to its original position on Peg A, which is equivalent to undoing the original move (i.e. first move the small ring from Peg A to Peg C and then move it from Peg C back to Peg A). This move would result in returning to state 1. Secondly, the small ring could be moved to Peg B, which would transform state 2 into state 3. Finally, the medium-sized ring could be moved from Peg A to Peg B, a move that would lead to a new state of the problem, state 4. In Figure 1.4 each of these moves is indicated by one of the lines emanating from state 2 of the problem. A line linking one state with another indicates the move possibilities between problem states. Thus, we could go from state 1 to state 2 (small ring from Peg A to Peg C) to state 4 (medium-sized ring from Peg A to Peg B) and back to state 2 (medium-sized ring from Peg B to Peg A) and then on to state 3 (small ring from Peg C to Peg

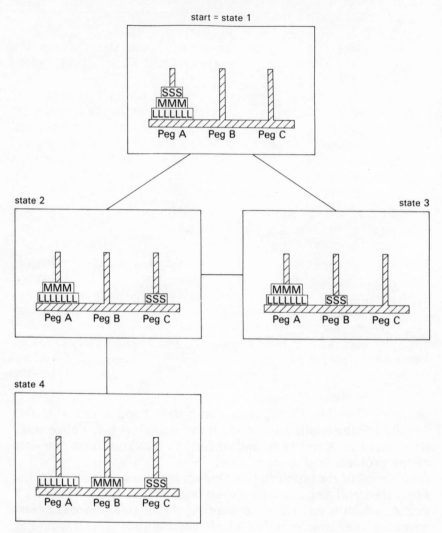

Figure 1.4

B) in the state space that has been developed so far. (If we made such a sequence of moves, we wouldn't be very good problem solvers, of course.)

SAQ 4
(a) Extend the state space on Figure 1.4 for the next possible move from state 3.
(b) List the states to which it is possible to go by moves from state 3.
(There are altogether twenty-seven states in the three-ring Towers of Hanoi problem. The entire state space will be given in the answer to this SAQ.)

26

Activity 2
Now consider the following problem, called the *Chinese Tea Ceremony problem* (adapted from Hayes and Simon, 1974). Spend a few minutes trying to solve it.

A most civilized and refined tea ceremony is practised in the inns of certain Himalayan villages. The ceremony involves a host and exactly two guests, neither more nor less. One of the guests is more senior in rank to the other guest. When his guests have arrived and have seated themselves at his table, the host performs three services for them. These services are listed below in the order of nobility which the Himalayans attribute to them.

Stoking the fire (least noble task)
Pouring the tea (medium nobility)
Reciting poetry (noblest task)

During the ceremony, any of those present may ask another person, 'Honoured Sir, may I perform this onerous task for you?'. However, a person may ask to do only the least noble of the tasks which the other is currently performing. Further, if a person is currently performing any tasks, then he may not ask to do a task which is nobler than the least noble task he is already performing. Custom requires that by the time the tea ceremony is over, all the tasks will have been transferred from the host to the more senior of the guests. How may this be accomplished?

SAQ 5
Fill in the details for the Chinese Tea Ceremony problem.

Initial state:

Goal state:

Operators:

Operator restrictions:

Did you recognize the similarities between the Chinese Tea Ceremony and the Towers of Hanoi problems? The 'three people' (Host, Junior Guest, and Senior Guest) in the Chinese Tea Ceremony problem are equivalent to the 'three pegs' in the Towers of Hanoi problem. The tasks are equivalent to rings. The degree of nobility of the different tasks is equivalent to the size of the three rings. The 'Ask' operator in the Chinese Tea Ceremony problem corresponds to the 'Move' operator in the Towers of Hanoi problem. In the Towers of Hanoi problem, no ring may be placed on top of a smaller one; in the Chinese Tea Ceremony problem no one can ask to perform a task 'nobler' than the least noble one he is currently performing. In the Towers of Hanoi problem the solver is *explicitly* told that only one ring may be moved at a time, but in the Chinese Tea Ceremony problem this particular operator restriction is implicit in the statement that 'a person may ask to do only the least noble of the tasks which the other is currently performing'.

How can we describe precisely the correspondences between the two different problems? This precision, as you may have suspected, can be achieved by drawing a complete diagram of move possibilities and states for both problems, and comparing the resulting state spaces. Note that the Towers of Hanoi and Chinese Tea Ceremony problems are both known as transformation problems because the rules specify operators (moves) for transforming each state to another state in a state space.

In Figure 1.5 the initial state of the Chinese Tea Ceremony problem is presented along with the equivalent representation of the initial state of the Towers of Hanoi problem. In Figure 1.5 the Junior Guest is represented as 'Guest (J)' and the Senior Guest as 'Guest (S)'. Also, 'R' stands for the task of 'reciting poetry', 'P' stands for 'pouring tea', and 'S' stands for 'stoking the fire'.

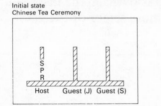 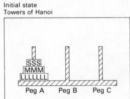

Figure 1.5

At the start of the Chinese Tea Ceremony problem, either of the guests can ask to perform the least noble task being performed by the Host, who is the only person performing tasks at the start of the problem. Figure 1.6 shows the results of performing these operations.

SAQ 6
What is the minimal number of moves needed to solve the Chinese Tea Ceremony problem? *Hint*: Look back to the answer to SAQ 1 (i.e., the Towers of Hanoi answer).

SAQ 7
The first few move possibilities in the Chinese Tea Ceremony problem are given in Figure 1.7. Fill in the blank boxes in states 6, 7, 8 and 9 with the states that would result from legal moves from state 4 and state 5.

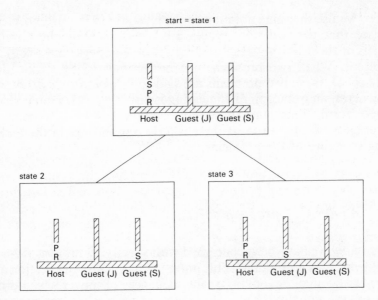

Figure 1.6

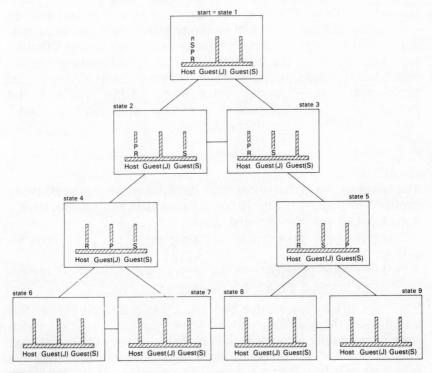

Figure 1.7

29

When we use the same notation to depict states in the two problems we see that the two state spaces are *identical*. Only the physical details of the problems (tasks or rings, people or pegs, and so on) are different. When two problems can be represented by an identical state space, these two problems are said to be *isomorphic problems*. In general, an isomorph of something is anything with similar structure or form. Thus, state space representations allow us to compare different problems, to see if there is a correspondence in the underlying structure of the problems.

3.2 Analysis of problem solving

Up to now we have been concerned with specifying the *structures* of problems in terms of all possible moves. However, in this section and the next we shall be looking at the sequences of moves which problem solvers actually choose. Using state space analysis the problem-solving behaviour of subjects can be analysed by looking at the paths which they follow through the state space of a problem. Paths through problems of related structures can be compared to see to what extent the basic problem structure affects subjects' behaviour and to what extent differences emerge as a result of the different superficial details of the problem statement. The following Activity and SAQ illustrate the point about different paths that different people take through a state space when solving problems, and provide you with an opportunity to practise what you know about constructing state space diagrams.

Activity 3
The following operators (moves) are involved in solving the everyday problem of making a cup of tea. Assume that you already have a cup, a pot of tea brewing, and so on:

ADD MILK TO CUP	= ADD MILK
STIR TEA	= STIR
ADD TEA TO CUP	= ADD TEA
ADD SUGAR TO CUP	= ADD SUGAR

The state space diagram for this activity is presented below. The initial state, the goal state and the states reachable from the initial state have already been filled in. The links between the initial state and its immediate successors have also been labelled with the operators that transform the initial state into the others. Fill in the

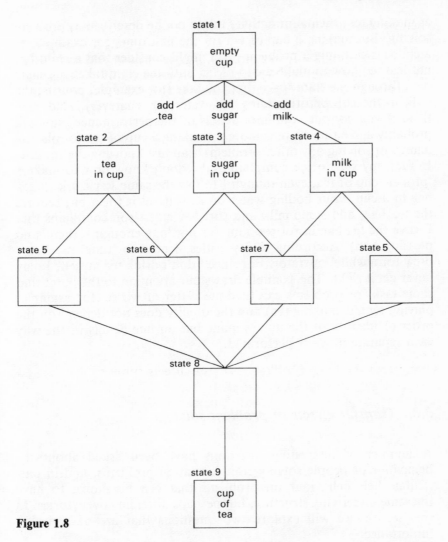

Figure 1.8

rest of the diagram with appropriate operator labels on the links and the resultant states. The answer appears on page 64.

SAQ 8
Mark the boxes representing the moves you as an individual problem solver (tea maker) would take through the state space.

You might want to complain that making a cup of tea is not really a problem. If you already know how to solve a problem, that is, if you have learned a routine for dealing with certain situations, such

31

as making tea, then your activity might not be described as problem solving. But making a cup of tea for the first time, for example, as a child, is certainly a problem. You might consider that a child has not learned how to make a cup of tea until the child takes the same path through the state space that you take (for example, pouring the milk in the cup before adding hot water, or whatever). And even then, if you consider the finer details of the performance, you will probably agree that there is more to making a cup of tea (or playing tennis, or solving any other problem) than just knowing the routine. In fact, my sons often complain that I don't know how to make a 'proper' cup of tea, even though I follow the same steps: stick a tea bag in a cup, pour boiling water on it, stare at it for a bit, remove the tea bag, add some milk and stir. My eldest son complains that I leave the tea bag in for too long (or not long enough – there's no pleasing him). According to my critics, I need to 'tune' my 'let it brew for a while' operator. But since I don't drink tea myself, I may never get it right. The example draws our attention to the point that some tasks or problems can be done better or worse (for example, playing tennis, making tea) and the quality does not depend on the order or identity of the moves made but on fine details of the way each separate move is performed.

3.3   Transfer effects in problem solving

A number of interesting questions have been asked about the behaviour of people solving transformation problems, and in particular their behaviour on problems that can be shown to have the same underlying structure, but perhaps different cover stories. In this section we will explore two questions that are of enduring importance.
1 Does experience on a given problem make it easier for subjects to solve new problems which are isomorphic (or nearly so) to the original problem (positive transfer)?
2 How do different kinds of task instructions affect the solution time and moves subjects choose to make through a state space?
In an attempt to provide an answer to the first question, Reed, Ernst and Banerji (1974) sought to discover whether skill acquired in performing one task could be transferred to an *analogous task* (similar, but not identical). The tasks they used were the Missionaries and Cannibals problem and the Jealous Husbands problem. The *Missionaries and Cannibals problem* is as follows:

Three missionaries and three cannibals seek to cross a river from the left bank to the right bank (as in Figure 1.9, below). They have a boat which can carry at most two people at a time. All missionaries and cannibals are able to navigate the boat. If at any time the cannibals outnumber the missionaries on either bank of the river, the missionaries will be eaten. Find the smallest number of crossings that will permit all the missionaries and cannibals to cross the river safely.

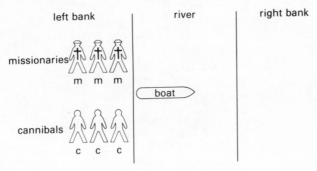

Figure 1.9

A state space diagram of the legal moves in the Missionaries and Cannibals problem is presented in Figure 1.10 overleaf.

The problem can be solved in eleven moves, but people seldom get a solution in the minimum number of moves. This is because the Missionaries and Cannibals problem contains a 'tricky state' (state 8). It's 'tricky' because in order to progress towards the goal the solver has to move one Missionary and one Cannibal from the right side of the river *back* to the left side, which seems counterintuitive because the move results in *fewer* Missionaries and Cannibals on the goal side of the river at state 9. People are very reluctant to make this move. This situation (state 9) is in fact quite like a previous state of the problem, state 4, in which two Missionaries and two Cannibals were on the left side of the river and one Missionary and one Cannibal on the right side. The crucial difference between these two states is the position of the boat. The move from state 1 of the problem to state 4 puts the boat on the right hand side of the river, while the move from state 8 to state 9 would leave the boat on the left hand side of the river.

The *Jealous Husbands problem* involves moving three men and their wives: in this respect it is quite analogous to the Missionaries and Cannibals problem. But, as the problem was posed by Reed *et al.*, an additional constraint was imposed: because the husbands

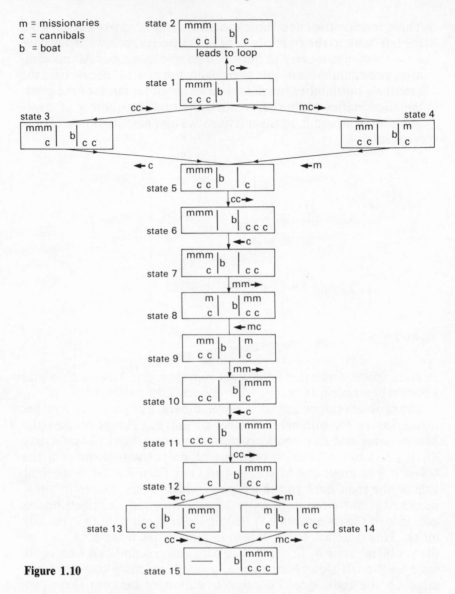

Figure 1.10

were jealous, a lone wife could not be left alone with a husband unless his own wife was present. In the Missionaries and Cannibals problem it doesn't make any difference which cannibals and missionaries are paired for a river crossing or which are left together on one bank or the other. Because of the restrictions concerning pairings of husbands and wives, the Jealous Husbands problem is harder than the Missionaries and Cannibals problem. Interestingly, both of these problems still have the same underlying structure when only legal moves are considered, but the Jealous Husbands problem has a lot more illegal move possibilities than the Missionaries and Cannibals problem. Problems with a similar but not identical structure are called *homomorphic problems*. Details of the experiment carried out by Reed *et al.* are provided in Techniques Box A.

TECHNIQUES BOX A

Reed, Ernst and Banerji (1974)

Rationale
Reed *et al.* predicted that subjects who are given problems with similar problem states would show improved performance on the second problem.

Method
Subjects were asked to solve two problems – either Missionaries and Cannibals and then Missionaries and Cannibals again, or Jealous Husbands and then Jealous Husbands again; or Missionaries and Cannibals and then Jealous Husbands or Jealous Husbands and then Missionaries and Cannibals. In addition, some subjects in the last two conditions were explicitly told about the relationship between the two problems. Data was collected on the total number of moves involved in solving each problem, and the number of illegal moves attempted.

Results
When subjects were presented with identical problems (Missionaries and Cannibals then Missionaries and Cannibals or Jealous Husbands then Jealous Husbands) there was improved performance in that fewer moves were required to solve the problem the second time. Subjects who were given the Jealous Husbands problem followed by the Missionaries and Cannibals problem improved their performance on the second problem only when the relationship between the two problems was revealed by the experimenter. Subjects who received the Missionaries and Cannibals problem followed by the more difficult Jealous Husbands problem showed no improvement even when the relationship was revealed by the experimenter.

The results from the Reed *et al.* experiment show that experience with a particular problem facilitates further attempts at solving the same problem again, but that this effect occurs only under certain circumstances for analogous problems. The special circumstances are (1) that the solver must first recognize or be told the relationship between analogous problems and (2) that the second problem should be somewhat simpler than the first, hence the subjects' failure to improve their performance on the Missionaries and Cannibals followed by Jealous Husbands problems even when the relationship was pointed out. These are surprising results in that they suggest that if people are left to themselves, they are not very good at bringing their previous experience to bear in solving related problems.

In another experiment, Luger and Bauer (1978) sought to discover whether skill acquired performing one task could be transferred to a second, identical (isomorphic) task, particularly where the tasks have a clear sub-problem structure.

The Towers of Hanoi problem has a pretty obvious sub-goal structure to it, as shown in its state space analysis, and most people, with a little experience on the problem, can work out what that structure is. The Towers of Hanoi problem can be broken down into sub-problems. For example, to solve the three-ring Towers of Hanoi problem it is necessary at some point to move the largest of the three rings from its original position on Peg A to Peg B. But before this can be done the two smaller rings must be assembled in their proper order on Peg C. The problem of moving two rings from one peg to another may be called a two-ring sub-problem, and constitutes a natural sub-part of the state space of the three-ring problem. Some people understand a lot about the Towers of Hanoi problem simply from reading its description. For instance, they don't usually move the same ring twice in succession – they don't take the small ring off Peg A and place it on Peg B, then take it off Peg B and place it on Peg C, because they understand just enough of the problem to see that this is a waste of time when the same effect could be achieved by simply taking the ring off Peg A and placing it directly on Peg C. They also rarely undo the last move they have made, for example, by taking the small ring off Peg A and placing it on Peg B and then taking it off Peg B and placing it right back on Peg A. Moves that subjects normally avoid reflect their limited understanding of the Towers of Hanoi problem when it is first presented to them. Other transformation problems, such as the Missionaries and Cannibals, do not have such an obvious problem structure.

In their experiment Luger and Bauer presented one group of subjects with the Towers of Hanoi problem followed by the Chinese Tea Ceremony problem, and another group with the Chinese Tea Ceremony problem followed by the Towers of Hanoi problem. Neither group of subjects was told that the two problems were related. Luger and Bauer argued that the isomorphic relationship between the two problems would lead to a transfer of learning, reflected in improved performance on the second task. They measured the total time both groups took to solve both problems as well as the number of states entered and the number of illegal moves attempted. The results confirmed their prediction about transfer of learning between the tasks in both conditions. These results show that identical problems with a clear sub-problem structure can enhance transfer of learning from one task to another. Luger and Bauer suggested that the lack of clear sub-problem structure in the Missionaries and Cannibals problem could account for the lack of transfer on the problems in the Reed *et al.* study. Taken together, these results also indicate that problem structure is important in determining problem difficulty.

The important issue of problem representation was investigated by Simon and Hayes (1976), who examined the consequences of different verbal formulations of a given problem in order to gain some insight into how problem statements are initially understood by problem solvers. Simon and Hayes used several isomorphic variations on the Towers of Hanoi problem. In some variations the rules of the problem specified legal moves in terms of size changes (for example, magically shrinking monsters). Other variations stuck to the idea of physically transferring items from one place to another. To give you some idea of the difficulties people experience in understanding problems with different cover stories but the same underlying structure, here is the statement of (a) a *transfer problem* and (b) a *change problem*, both of which were used in studies by Simon and Hayes.

(a)   a transfer problem

Three five-handed extraterrestrial monsters were holding three crystal globes. Because of the quantum-mechanical peculiarities of their neighbourhood, both monsters and globes came in exactly three sizes – small, medium and large – and no other sizes were permitted. The medium-sized monster was holding the small globe; the small monster was holding the large globe; and the large monster was holding the medium-sized globe. Since this situation offended their keenly developed sense of symmetry, they proceeded to transfer globes from one another so that each monster would have a globe proportionate to its own size. Monster etiquette complicated the solution to the problem because it required that:

1 only one globe could be transferred at one time;
2 if a monster was holding two globes, only the larger of the two could be transferred;
3 a globe could not be transferred to a monster who was holding a larger globe.

By what sequence of transfers could the monster have solved this problem?

(b)   a change problem

Three five-handed extraterrestrial monsters were holding three crystal globes. Because of the quantum-mechanical peculiarities of their neighbourhood, both monsters and globes came in exactly three sizes – small, medium and large – and no other sizes were permitted. The medium-sized monster was holding the small globe; the small monster was holding the large globe; and the large monster was holding the medium-sized globe. Since this situation offended their keenly developed sense of symmetry, they proceeded to shrink and expand the globes so that each monster would have a globe proportionate to its own size. Monster etiquette complicated the solution to the problem because it required that:

1 only one globe could be shrunk or expanded at a time:
2 if two globes were of the same size, only the globe held by the larger monster could be shrunk or expanded;
3 a globe could not be shrunk or expanded to the same size as the globe of a larger monster.

By what sequence of transfers could the monsters have solved this problem?

Simon and Hayes presented different group of subjects with either:
1 a transfer problem and then a change problem;
2 a change problem and then a transfer problem;
3 two transfer problems which differed according to whether the monster was the agent (instigator) of the transfer or the patient (recipient) of the transfer;
4 two change problems which differed according to whether the monster was the agent or the patient of the change.

The results showed that transfer problems were solved in about half the time needed to solve the change problems. Improved performance on the second of each pair of problems was much more evident when the same basic problem was used (that is, transfer-patient *versus* transfer-agent) than when there was a switch from 'transfer' to 'change' or vice versa. All variations had a strong influence on the representations adopted by the subjects when they attempted to solve the problems (as revealed by their verbal protocols). The results showed that problem structure alone, as reflected in the state space, was not enough to predict the kind of difficultiies a subject might have in solving a problem. The task of 'understanding' the problem itself, that is, of adopting some internal representation of the states and operators, would have a drastic effect on the solution process, because some representation might involve much simpler processing operations than others.

Hayes and Simon (1974) have also constructed a computer program called UNDERSTAND which simulates the process of building internal representations that differ for different task instructions.

Summary of Section 3

- A state space analysis of a problem provides us with a representation of the underlying structure of a problem.
- A state space diagram depicts all possible transformations between all legal states of a problem, connected by legal moves (operators).
- State space diagrams can be used as a tool for determining the relationship between the structures of two or more problems. Problems which can be represented with identical state space diagrams are called isomorphic or problem isomorphs.
- Problem-solving strategies can be analysed in terms of the paths of moves taken by an individual solver through a state space.
- Experimental studies on transformation problems such as Missionaries and Cannibals and Jealous Husbands show that experience on a problem does not necessarily transfer to another problem of the same type unless people are aware of the similarity and the second problem is simpler than the first.
- Structural factors, such as problems having an identical and clear state space structure, and psychological factors, such as instructions and the number of mental steps involved in solving the problem, both have an effect on problem-solving strategies.

4   Simon's information processing theory of problem solving

The next few pages are devoted to an overview of the information processing theory of human problem solving put forward by Simon (1978), reprinted in Aitkenhead and Slack (1985). Simon's theory characterizes problem solving as an interaction between a task environment (that is, a problem) and a problem solver, who is thought of as an information-processing system.

Simon points out that understanding the important properties of a problem (which he calls a *task environment*) is as important in understanding problem solving as understanding the characteristics of the information processing system that does the solving. The problem structure itself constrains the processes of problem solving in that it contains considerable information about what the problem is and what needs to be done in order to solve the problem. As we have seen in previous sections, problems often contain information about the initial state of the problem, the goal, and the operators that can be used to achieve the goal. Problem information also often rules out certain actions: for example, in the Towers of Hanoi problem the operator restrictions rule out the possibility of simply moving the whole tower of rings over in one move. This is not to claim that people always perfectly understand the tasks with which they find themselves confronted, or that they will invariably be able to solve problems even given that they have a perfect understanding of what the problem is. The claim is simply that people approach problems rationally (to the extent that they are capable of rationality) and that problems themselves contain a lot of information that can be used to guide solution processes.

In order to solve problems people must construct a *mental representation* of the given problem information: initial state, goal, operators and operator restrictions. Simon refers to this mental representation of the problem as the person's *problem space*. What we have referred to in Section 3 as a state space Simon calls a *basic problem space*, that is, an omniscient observer's view of the structure of a problem. It is important to keep this distinction in mind: the problem space is a person's individual representation of a problem, and as such may contain more or less information than that given in the problem statement. For example, when you read the Towers of Hanoi problem description you presumably *inferred* that you could look at the coins as you moved them from one circle to another although the description of the problem contained no information either permitting or forbidding 'watching what you are doing'. In fact, many problem descriptions contain such implicit information, for example, the psychology examination situation referred to on page 21. Thus, an essential idea behind the notion of a person's individual problem space as discussed by Simon is that when confronted with a problem people bring to bear that part of their total store of knowledge that is (or that they think is) relevant to the problem at hand. People try to relate what they understand about a particular problem to specific knowledge they have about problems of that type.

During the course of solving a problem a solver progresses through a sequence of *knowledge states*. A knowledge state contains the information a person has available at each point in the problem solving process, or which can be made available (for example, by retrieving knowledge from long-term memory). Transformation of a knowledge state is accomplished by applying *mental operations* to change it into another knowledge state. You have probably noticed that the terminology used by Simon is very similar to the way we described state space analysis of problems in terms of states and operations for moving from one state to the next. The crucial difference is that we are now talking not about the objective structure of a problem but about *mental* knowledge states and *mental* operations going on inside the problem solver's head. This has the important effect of allowing for individual differences between problem solvers.

People differ in the way they solve problems (the sequence of mental states visited during the solution to the problem) for a number of reasons. People differ in the amount of experience they have had with a particular type of problem; they employ different strategies in solving a particular type of problem; and they also differ because they pay attention to different aspects of the problem structure. I have already stressed that people differ in the way they represent problems. The way a person represents a problem has powerful determining effects on the ease with which a problem can be solved, or even whether it can be solved at all. Hayes (1978) uses the following pair of examples to illustrate this point.

Activity 4
Consider an ordinary, 64-square checkerboard in which the squares in two diagonally opposite corners have been removed, as in Figure 1.11 (overleaf). If you had 31 dominoes, each of which would cover exactly two squares on the checkerboard, is there any way you could arrange the dominoes so that all the remaining 62 squares would be covered? If you think you could, how would you prove it? And if you think not, how would you prove that?

Most people find that a hard problem, especially the proof. The problem is easier to solve (and prove) if it is presented in more everyday terms.

Activity 5
Imagine that you are a matchmaker, and that you have been summoned to some remote village which contains exactly 64 unmarried young people, 32 men and 32 women. Your job is to pair up the couples in time for a group wedding two days hence, a Saturday morning. You work throughout the day and all day Friday, when you eventually succeed in matching couples to the satisfaction of everybody concerned. But, that evening, during pre-wedding

Figure 1.11

celebrations, two of the men get into a fight and kill one another. Can all of the 62 remaining young people get married on Saturday morning as planned?

You can use your solution to the problem in Activity 5 as a basis for solving the problem about the mutilated checkerboard, if you haven't solved it already. The checkerboard contains squares of alternating colours. Every white square is bordered by a black square. A domino placed on two squares must by necessity cover a black square and a white square. But in the mutilated checkerboard two black squares are missing. Hence, the 62 remaining squares cannot be covered by 31 dominoes. Simon points out that people do not always construct an optimal representation of a problem. But the way a problem is presented can help them to achieve a more useful representation.

Problem solving is also influenced by properties of the information-processing system, such as the capacity of working memory and the amount of time involved in storage and retrieval processes in long-term memory. If working memory is only capable

of holding a few units of information and optimal performance on a task requires that more states and rules need to be considered, then performance will be less than optimal. Consider having to remember a telephone number just long enough to dial it. Read the number that follows this sentence (once only) and then try to repeat it back immediately. 9376054. Now let's make the problem a bit harder. Imagine that you find a message asking you to call someone at a particular number. Read the name and the number that follow this sentence (again, once only) and then try to repeat them back, in the same order. Mr Kresge, General Insurance Company, 2585492. Although working memory capacity limits performance, the limitation is considered to present only very general constraints on problem-solving performance in that a solver may extend the capacity of short-term memory by writing and referring to notes or intermediate results during the course of problem solving.

All the facts a person knows, and procedures for solving problems, are stored in long-term memory, and the facts and procedures that different people have acquired obviously have an effect on the way they solve problems. Also important are interactions between working memory and long-term memory. Kotovsky *et al.* (1985) have shown that people are unable to plan a sequence of moves on puzzle-like problems until they have spent a considerable amount of time in learning problem rules and practising rule application. During practice people 'overlearn' or automate the rule application process (that is, the rules are stored in long-term memory and are made readily accessible when required). Thus, some of the burden on working memory is shifted to long-term memory.

Information-processing psychologists have been strongly influenced by research in *artificial intelligence (AI)*. AI researchers design computer programs that perform activities such as 'seeing', language understanding, or problem solving. AI researchers are interested in getting their programs to work, and to work efficiently, without being concerned with the way humans perform such tasks (although they are willing to use any available knowledge about human performance). Research in AI has shown that computers have to be loaded with vast amounts of information (of many different kinds) in order to get them to perform tasks of any complexity. They have also demonstrated the importance of the organization of knowledge — how to represent vast amounts of information in such a way that it can be retrieved when it is needed. This problem is especially hard when you consider that AI researchers (and people) cannot always predict the way in which stored information will be used in future.

Information-processing psychologists such as Simon argue that a supreme test of the theory of cognitive behaviour is to specify the theory in such detail that it can be implemented as a computer program which actually performs the behaviour the theory is trying to account for. To quote Polson and Jeffries (1982):

> 'Unlike a theory presented as descriptive prose, a process model of a task requires the concrete specification of the actions and decisions that a solver performs. Consider, for example, the selection of potential moves. A less specific theory might merely state that a move is selected for consideration, whereas the computer formalism forces us to decide the order in which moves are chosen. We can do this at different levels of detail, however. We can specify an order, which becomes a testable tenet of the theory.'

Constructing a program that solves problems, even one that seems to display the same characteristics in solving problems as human solvers, demonstrates only one way in which the problem could be solved. But a running program does not constitute proof that the mechanisms embodied in the program are the same mechanisms that underlie human performance. Other programs, with different mechanisms, might also mimic human performance. In such cases various criteria must be used to decide between the models as embodied in computer programs. Programs that embody models of human peformance are often tested by comparing the step by step performance of the program with the step by step performance of a human solver. Data on human performance may be gathered by collecting a verbal account from the person solving the problem, known as a *verbal protocol.*

A major advantage of a computer simulation of human problem solving is that it forces a theorist to be completely explicit about the information a problem solver uses and how that information is organized in memory. It also forces the theorist to be precise in specifying the processes that operate on stored information, and the control structure of the processing system – how processes are selected from one moment to the next.

4.1   Heuristic search

Given that problem solving is characterized as mental transformations of problem states, a solver is always in the position of having to choose an operator for transforming a current knowledge state. One way to proceed from any knowledge state would simply be to apply all possible legal operators in order to generate all possible successor states, and to choose one of the successors as a new starting point for making further progress in the problem. Unfortunately, most problem spaces are quite large − even the simple three-ring Towers of Hanoi problem has a total of twenty-seven different states − and human working memory capacity is severely limited. People are unable to keep this much information in mind. In order to get around these limitations, people employ various *strategies* for guiding a search for solutions to problems.

The selection and evaluation of mental operators are characterized in Simon's theory as *heuristic search processes*. *Heuristics* are rule-of-thumb, problem-solving methods which often succeed but which do not guarantee a solution to a problem. A mundane example of a heuristic is, 'Ask for directions when lost in an unfamiliar place'. Asking local people how to get from one place to another and following their directions often does the trick; but you could follow a guide's instructions perfectly and still end up on the wrong side of a city if your guide was mistaken about the location of the place you wanted to get to or set out to mislead you. Heuristics are usually contrasted with *algorithms* or procedures which guarantee success if followed faithfully. The rules of arithmetic are good examples of algorithms.

4.2   Means-ends analysis

Many problems with a clearly defined goal state, which of course include transformation problems, can be solved using a general problem-solving strategy called *means-ends analysis*. The method was developed by Newell, Shaw and Simon (1958) in the *General Problem Solving* computer program (called *GPS*). Although many versions of GPS were designed only with the goal of making machines perform 'intelligently', some versions were designed with human performance limitations in mind. In a comparison of GPS with human problem solving on transformation problems, Newell and Simon (1972) concluded that much of human behaviour could be characterized in terms of means-ends analysis.

Means-ends analysis works by determining *differences* between a current state of a problem and a goal state − differences between what you have now and what you want to end up with — and selecting operators known to be useful in reducing such differences. The basic idea behind means-ends analysis is that people have knowledge about the *means* (operators) at their disposal for achieving certain *ends*, or goals. Think of the various means you know about for achieving a goal such as 'getting down to the shops'. You could walk, drive your car, ride a bicycle, run, roller skate, or take a bus. To see how means-ends analysis can help to build up a plan, consider the following (invented) protocol of me building a plan.

My goal or *end* is to transform 'me at home' into 'me in Trafalgar Square'. The first task is to compare these two states and find the difference between them. I find the difference to be one of 'location'. The *means* I have of reducing differences of location are *operators*, such as 'walk' or 'go by train'. Some operators, for example, walk, can be rejected as not feasible, because I live fifty miles away in Milton Keynes and I am extremely lazy; but 'go by train' is feasible, so my next goal is to apply this operator to the initial state, 'me at home'. Unfortunately the operator will not apply immediately because the conditions are not right — trains don't stop at my house. If I want to take a train I have to get to Milton Keynes Central station. So I set up a new *sub-goal* to reduce the difference between 'me at home' and 'me at Milton Keynes Central station'. Again the difference is one of location and so again I refer to 'travel' operators. I can reject 'walk' as not feasible (I am lazy) and 'go by train' as a potential loop (I am already considering going by train from my home) and select 'go by taxi'. This cannot be applied because the conditions are wrong – the taxi driver doesn't know I need him. The difference is one of information, so I look for an operator which can reduce differences of information and find communication operators, such as, 'use the telephone'...

Means-ends analysis works, then, by analysing problems into goals and sub-goals by working out which moves (means) will attain the end goal (means-ends analysis). Operators are selected that are known to be useful for achieving particular goals and sub-goals. This kind of analysis can be carried on to any required depth and will eventually produce a plan consisting of a sequence of *operators* which can be applied directly: walk into the kitchen, telephone for a taxi, be carried in the taxi to the train station, walk from the taxi into the station, and so on and so forth, until I find myself in Trafalgar Square.

Means-ends analysis is a very general problem-solving method, useful in a large number of problem-solving situations, including real-world situations involving considerable amounts of knowledge, such as the example just given. In order to plan a trip from, say, London to Pittsburgh, a solver needs to know a great deal about travel agencies, airports, money, and numerous other things. However, means-ends analysis may not always be the best way of solving any particular problem. In certain circumstances it can even lead people away from a solution to a problem, as we shall see in Section 5.

4.3   Protocol analysis

In order to obtain information about people's individual problem-solving strategies, unique methods are needed to gather data that allows us to make inferences about what is going on inside people's heads while they are working on a problem. One method that is sometimes used for gathering data is to collect a *verbal protocol*. Such protocols result from asking subjects to 'think aloud' while solving a problem, just as you were asked to do when attempting the problem presented in Activity 1. These verbalizations, plus whatever actions a person takes in solving a problem, are recorded and analysed phrase by phrase. Each phrase represents an assertion about the task or a single act of task-specific behaviour.

In order to illustrate protocol analysis, consider the fragment of a protocol presented in Table 1.1 (overleaf). A first pass analysis of the first half of the protocol has been provided, to give you an idea of how such an analysis proceeds. The numbered lines contain the statements made by the subject, and the comments in brackets indicate the kind of mental processes that seem to be reflected in the preceding statements. This protocol is slightly bogus because:

1 it was taken by the same person who was doing the problem;
2 he was writing down the protocol instead of taping and transcribing it;
3 the person is a psychologist who happens to be studying learning and problem solving.

The goal of the first pass analysis is to identify the processes that occur. On a second pass the analyst might search for patterns among the processes identified on the first pass.

If you made a record of your thoughts in solving the Activity 1 problem, then you know what it is like to try to provide a researcher with a verbal protocol. In fact, obtaining a good verbal protocol from a subject is a difficult task. For one thing, subjects may report something different from what they actually did in an attempt to justify themselves. Many subjects find it difficult to speak out their spontaneous thought processes in the presence of another person or a tape recorder. In this situation, many of the thoughts are simply unavailable for study because they remain unspoken.

More worrying are the arguments of Nisbett and Wilson (1977), who claim that protocols are spurious evidence for cognitive processes because subjects do not have introspective access to the higher mental processes involved in problem solving. They argue that protocols are after-the-event rationalizations in which subjects offer hypotheses to explain what they are doing. However, because they have no access to their own thought processes, the subjects' reports

Table 1.1

The problem
On Monday morning I had $132.48 in my account. During the week I made the following transactions:

Cheque $12.25; Deposit 31.80; Cheque 20.15; Cheque 15.83.

What's my balance now?

---

1 So, let's isolate the cheques to see how much I lost.
  (apply 'divide into like parts' – heuristic: cheques and deposit)
2 Twenty-five and fifteen is forty...
  (divide into cents part and dollars part sub-problems)
  (automatic, double column, well rehearsed (fives) addition process)
3 plus eighty-three...
  (set up sub-problem for harder addition)
4 is three [3]...
  (fast zero addition)
5 four and eight is twelve ...
  (addition fact recall)
6 so that's one twenty-three [1.23]...
  (finish sub-problem) (begin sub-problem for dollars part)
7 twelve, twenty and fifteen is, let's see, thirty-five...
  (fast addition 20 + 15 = 35)
8 plus...forty-seven...
  (fast addition 35 + 12 = 47) (finish sub-problem)
9 plus one twenty-three is forty-seven twenty-three.
  (Combine...but forgot to add on 1.00!)
10 Now that minus thirty-one eighty is how much I subtract...
  (do the other half of the top goal division).
11 so forty-seven twenty-three, less thirty-one eighty...
  (sets up subtraction problem: 47.23 − 31.80 = ??)
12 three...zero...three
13 two...eight
14 carry...no borrow... twelve...twelve
15 eight...four
16 seven...
17 no six
18 ...less one...five
19 four...three.
20 Do I have to borrow again?...No.
21 Four...three...one.
22 OK so one thirty-two forty-eight less fifteen forty-three is...
23 five cents.
24 Thirty minus fifteen plus two is fifteen...
25 seventeen, so...
26 it's one seventeen and five cents.

---

are no more valid than the speculations of an external observer. In support of their view, Nisbett and Wilson cite numerous instances of introspections concerned with perception, emotion, and problem solving where subjects are either unable to verbalize their reasoning, or are clearly inaccurate in doing so.

In defending the use of verbal protocols Ericsson and Simon (1980) have outlined two crucial issues:

1 Do verbal protocols accurately reflect underlying cognitive processes?

2 Does the production of a verbal protocol significantly distort the normal processes?

Ericsson and Simon argue that a protocol can be validated if there is a close correspondence between the statements in the protocol and the subjects' behaviour. We constantly use this method in everyday situations. If someone said to you 'Wow, I'm hungry as a horse', then you expect that person to perform some action that will lead him to a meal. In the laboratory, if we ask someone to tell us what he is thinking about when he solves, say, an algebra problem, we have not only his comments about what he is doing but also the partial working and final results of his calculations, which can be used to verify his comments on what he was thinking about at different steps through the solution. Ericsson and Simon admit that the accuracy of a verbal protocol can be affected by the nature of the task. A high level of reliability is achieved when subjects report the current contents of short-term memory, rather than base the report on information stored in long-term memory which can be distorted by other stored knowledge. This means that accuracy of reporting is highest when it occurs at the same time, that is, is concurrent with the task rather than retrospectively, and the amount of prompting by the experimenter is minimized. The performance of subjects on problem-solving tasks with and without concurrent reporting was compared by Ericsson and Simon; they concluded from their findings that verbal protocols do not significantly influence performance in most instances.

What other factors might influence the accuracy of verbal protocols? Some of the cognitive processes underlying problem solving will be 'automatic', and by definition, unconscious and so will not be open to introspection. 'Pattern recognition processes' are automatic, for example, and we wouldn't expect subjects to be able to talk about such processes. The best we can hope for is information in a subject's statements that permits us to infer that particular mental processes occur in a given task situation.

Summary of Section 4

- Information-processing psychologists such as Simon view problem solving as search through a mental problem space.
- Problem solvers bring their own knowledge to bear in constructing problem spaces and in searching for solutions to problems. Heuristics are (imperfect) rules of thumb that guide search for a solution to a problem.
- Means-ends analysis is a powerful heuristic which involves breaking a problem down into goals and sub-goals until a point is reached at which specific actions can be taken to solve a problem.
- Verbal protocols are used to externalize a subject's internal problem-solving strategies. Although verbal protocols are not a complete record of the internal processes involved in problem solving, they do provide invaluable information about them.

5 Polson's model of transformation problems

In an early analysis of problem solving on transformation problems (the Hobbits and Orcs problem, an isomorph of the Missionaries and Cannibals problem), Thomas (1974) suggested that people are able to plan three or four steps ahead when working out their solution because he observed that subjects spent a long time thinking before making some moves, and then a cluster of moves was made in rapid succession. Thomas argued that a planning process occurred during the time subjects were thinking about the problem, and that when the plan was completed it was executed quickly.

Over the past several years a group of investigators based at the University of Colorado has presented a series of computer models of human performance on transformation problems (Atwood and Polson, 1976; Jeffries, Polson, Razran and Atwood, 1977; Atwood, Masson and Polson, 1980). The 'Polson model', as I shall refer to the collected efforts of the authors of the various papers, is based on the premise that people have, at best, only a limited understanding of the structure of difficult transformation problems when they are first confronted with them. Polson argues that, because of this limited understanding, and because of memory limitations, people are not able to plan a sequence of moves in solving such problems.

Activity 6
The Waterjug Problem   Imagine that you are given an 8-litre jug, a 5-litre jug, and a 3-litre jug. At the start of the problem the 8-litre jug is full of water, and both the 5- and the 3-litre jugs are empty (see Figure 1.12, 'Initial state').

Initial state   Goal state

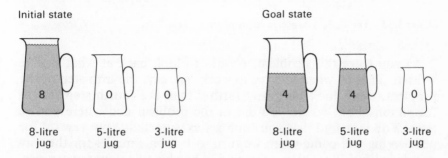

| 8-litre
jug | 5-litre
jug | 3-litre
jug | | 8-litre
jug | 5-litre
jug | 3-litre
jug |

Figure 1.12

Can you find some way of pouring the water back and forth between the jugs so that you end up with 4 litres of water in the 8-litre jug and the other 4 litres in the 5-litre jug? There are no markings on any of the jugs, so you have to work by filling empty jugs to capacity or by emptying the contents of one jug into another having a larger capacity. So, to start off you would have to fill either the 5-litre jug or the 3-litre jug from the 8-litre jug. Your task is to solve the problem with the minimum number of moves.

Make a record of your attempts at solving this problem. Get a piece of paper and write '8-litre jug', '5-litre jug' and '3-litre jug' at the top of the page, as in line 1 of Figure 1.13 overleaf. On line 2 indicate the contents of each jug at the start of the problem: 8, 0 and 0. Then, on subsequent lines, after you decide what action to take, fill in the new contents of each jug. If you decide to pour from the 8-litre jug into the 5-litre jug as a first step, you would indicate this by writing on the next line, '3' for the new contents of the 8-litre jug, '5' for the new contents of the 5-litre jug, and 0 for the unchanged contents of the 3-litre jug. This step is indicated on line 3 in Figure 1.13. The figure also shows the result of the next step, in which the solver pours from the 5-litre jug into the 3-litre jug which leaves 3 litres of water in the 8-litre jug, 2-litres of water in the 5-litre jug and 3 litres of water in the 3-litre jug. (I am not, of course, suggesting that these are necessarily the first two steps in solving the problem.)

	8-litre jug	5-litre jug	3-litre jug
line 1			
line 2	8	0	0
line 3	3	5	0
line 4	3	2	3
line 5			
line 6			
line 7			
line 8			
etc.			
etc.			

Figure 1.13 The 8, 5, 3 Waterjugs problem

As you solve this problem, try not to look back at what you've written. That is, when you try to work out, say, the fifth step of the problem, don't look back any farther than the fourth step for information about where you are in the problem and where you've been. You may find that you soon get exasperated. Your reward for persevering will come when we turn to Polson's model for the way people solve this problem, as you will be able to compare your performance with the performance of Polson's subjects.

It would be nice if you could also persuade a friend to solve the problem. Keep a record of each step in your friend's solution. Ask your friend to tell you what he or she is thinking about while working on the problem. See if you recognize any of the same difficulties you yourself experienced in solving the problem.

SAQ 9
(a) What is the minimum number of steps needed to solve the 8, 5, 3 Waterjugs problem?
(b) How many steps did you take in solving the problem?
(c) Write a few lines describing your own strategies in solving the problem. What was the major source of difficulty for you in solving the problem?

5.1   Performance limitations

The 8, 5, 3 Waterjugs problem is difficult partly because its underlying structure is tricky, as we shall see presently. The underlying structure of the problem is not as transparent as the structure of the Towers of Hanoi problem. On the surface, it might seem reasonable to set up some intermediate sub-goal, such as isolating 1 litre of water in either the 8- or the 5-litre jug, and then adding the contents of the 3-litre jug to the isolated 1 litre. But it is not easy to see how to work out a series of moves that would isolate 1 litre of water.

A second reason why the problem is hard is because of the load it imposes on working memory. In the ideal case, solving the problem involves assembling a lot of information about possible moves to different states of the problem. Polson argues that the capacity of working memory limits the amount of planning that can be accomplished. In order to see Polson's point, consider one strategy you might use in planning a sequence of moves from a current state of the Waterjug problem. The strategy we will consider is simply working out each possible move from a current state. At the start of the problem (assume that you represent the 8-litre jug in memory as Jug 8, and so on) the solver needs to remember:

Jug 8 contents 8
Jug 5 contents 0
Jug 3 contents 0

The legal moves from the initial state of the problem are the following:

1 Pour the contents of Jug 8 into Jug 5
2 Pour the contents of Jug 8 into Jug 3
3 Pour the contents of Jug 5 into Jug 8 ╱
4 Pour the contents of Jug 5 into Jug 3 ╱
5 Pour the contents of Jug 3 into Jug 8
6 Pour the contents of Jug 3 into Jug 5

If you considered each of these possibilities, and tried to store each of them, you would have to remember all of the following information (although not in this exact form, of course):

Jug 8 contents 8
Jug 5 contents 0
Jug 3 contents 0

Jug 8 goal contents 4
Jug 5 goal contents 4

If I pour the contents of Jug 8 into Jug 5, the result would be:

Jug 8 contents 3
Jug 5 contents 5
Jug 3 contents 0

If I pour the contents of Jug 8 into Jug 3, the result would be:

Jug 8 contents 5
Jug 5 contents 0
Jug 3 contents 3

I can't pour the contents of Jug 5 into either Jug 3 or Jug 8 because Jug 5 is empty.

I can't pour the contents of Jug 3 into either Jug 5 or Jug 8 because Jug 3 is empty.

Even if you write some of this down, it is still a lot of information.

And of course this is not yet the whole story. Once the possible transformations have been worked out you would have to determine which of the moves to make. Even then you would have worked out only the first step in the plan. In order to work out the next step you would have to keep information about the current state:

Jug 8 contents 8
Jug 5 contents 0
Jug 3 contents 0

as well as information about the first move you intend to make, which, for the sake of argument, might be:

Pour the contents of Jug 8 into Jug 5.

Of course, you would also have to keep in mind the state that would result from making the intended move:

Jug 8 contents 3 litres
Jug 5 contents 5 litres
Jug 3 contents 0 litres

Next you would have to work out all the possible succeeding states from the second state, evaluate them, decide on a move, remember what the move is, and remember what the next state would be in order to work out the third move. Even using paper and pencil to write down your moves and outcomes there is still a great deal of information to keep track of when planning your next moves.

Because of these considerations – human memory capacity and lack of complete problem understanding – Polson argues that a solver works out a solution to such problems one step at a time. The strategy used for evaluating and selecting moves is based on means-ends analysis and memory processes.

5.2 Move selection processes

This is how the process works. You have three different capacity jugs to work with: 8, 5 and 3 litres. Your *goal* is to end up with 4 litres of water in the 8-litre jug and 4 litres of water in the 5-litre jug. At the start of the problem the 8-litre jug contains 8 litres of water and the 5-litre jug contains 0 litres of water. There are two legal moves from the initial state: either pour 5 litres of water into the 5-litre jug or else pour 3 litres of water into the 3-litre jug. Which move should you take? This question raises the problems of determining how close you are to the goal now, and of determining which move (out of the legal possibilities) would bring you closer to the goal.

Initial state

Capacity of the jugs:	8-litre jug	5-litre jug	3-litre jug
Contents of the jugs:	8	0	0
Goal contents of the jugs:	4	4	0
Difference:	4	4 = 8	

Goal state

Capacity of the jugs:	8-litre jug	5-litre jug	3-litre jug
Contents of the jugs:	4	4	0
Goal contents of the jugs:	4	4	0
Difference:	0	0 = 0	

Figure 1.14   Means-ends values for the initial and goal states of the 8, 5, 3 Water-jugs problem

Consider the initial state of the problem, referring to the contents of Figure 1.14.

What's the difference between what the solver wants and what he has at the start of the problem? There are two differences. First, the 8-litre jug contains 4 litres too much water, and, second, the 5-litre jug contains 4 litres too little water (as in the initial state portion of Figure 1.14). If we ignore any minus signs and 'add up' the differences between what we have and what we want, it can be seen that the solver is 8 'units' of distance away from the goal at the start of the 8, 5, 3 problem. Note that according to this scheme the third jug is not considered at all. This is because the solver is presumed to be always trying to get closer to the goal of having 4 litres in the 8-litre jug and 4 litres in the 5-litre jug. The contents of the goal jugs are the focus of the solver's problem-solving efforts.

When the problem is solved, as indicated in the goal state portion of Figure 1.14, there will be 0 units of distance to the goal. You should note that Polson does not intend to suggest that we have this particular form of an evaluation function stored in our heads; rather that the evaluation function captures the essence of the means-ends strategy which subjects use when confronted with a problem such as this.

How can means-ends analysis help to determine which move to take from any state in the problem? You need to work out the move possibilities from the current state and choose a move that brings you closer to the goal state. Figure 1.15 presents evaluations for the only two legal moves from the initial state of the problem: (A) filling the 5-litre jug or (B) filling the 3-litre jug. The first option would lead you to state 3, 5, 0, where the numbers indicate the next contents of each jug in order, while the second option would lead to state 5, 0, 3.

In terms of distance from the goal state, the evaluations indicate that the best initial move to make would be to go to state 3,5,0. This

Initial state			
Capacity of the jugs:	8-litre jug	5-litre jug	3-litre jug
Contents of the jugs:	8	0	0
(A) Move possibility number one: Pour 5 litres from the 8-litre jug into the 5-litre jug.			
Next state			
Contents of the jugs:	3	5	0
Goal contents of the jugs:	4	4	0
	—	—	—
Difference:	1	1 = 2	
(B) Move possibility number two: Pour 3 litres from the 8-litre jug into the 3-litre jug.			
Next state			
Contents of the jugs:	5	0	3
Goal contents of the jugs:	4	4	0
	—	—	—
Difference:	1	4 = 5	

Figure 1.15 Means-ends values assigned to each of the two move possibilities from the initial state of the 8, 5, 3 Waterjugs problem.

transformation would leave you only 2 units of distance from the goal, with one too few litres of water in the 8-litre jug and one too many litres in the 5-litre jug. (Was this your first move?) The other alternative – a move to state 5,0,3 – has a value of 5 units of distance from the goal.

There are two different solution paths through the state space for this problem, as shown in Figure 1.16. The initial state is labelled 'S' on the graph. The states that can be reached from the start state are labelled 'L' (for first state on the left-hand solution path) and 'R' (for first state on the right-hand solution path). The means-ends value for all states is presented in slash marks at the side of the state information (/5/ for state 'L' and /2/ for state 'R').

From both states 'L' and 'R' there are exactly three possible moves. The first move is a loop; it undoes the previous move and leads the solver back to the initial state 8, 0, 0 of the problem. Another possible move from the first state on either solution path leads to the 'transition' state which links the two solution paths (state 0, 5, 3, marked 'T' on the graph). Finally, one forward move is available from either state 'L' or state 'R', leading to state 5, 3, 0 or state 3, 2, 3 respectively.

From all states except the four marked 'S', 'L', 'R' and 'T' at the top of the graph, there are exactly four move possibilities. There is

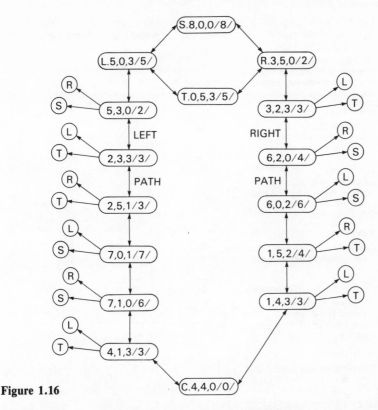

Figure 1.16

always the possibility of a move to the immediately previous state and a move to a new state of the problem. The other two move possibilities always lead the solver back to one of the four states at the top of the graph, as indicated by the labels pointed to in the ovals at the sides of the remaining states. Details of the move possibilities from the second state on the right-hand solution path (state 3, 2, 3) are presented in Figure 1.17, which you can compare to the information in Figure 1.16.

What would happen if a solver used only means-ends analysis to solve the problem? In order to find out, consider the means-ends values for successive states in Figure 1.16. The states on the right-hand solution path have the following values: 2, 3, 4, 6, 4 and 3. On the left-hand path the values are: 5, 2, 3, 3, 7, 6 and 3. On the right-hand solution path, things seem to get steadily worse after the first move, until at state 6, 0, 2, with a means-ends value of 6, the solver is seemingly almost as badly off as at the start of the problem. On the left-hand path things seem to get slightly better after the first move, until the solver suddenly reaches state 7, 0, 1 with a means-ends value of 7. Things seem to be really getting out of hand at these

State 3, 2, 3

	8-litre jug	5-litre jug	3-litre jug
Capacity of the jugs:			
Contents of the jugs:	3	2	3

(A) Move possibility number one: Pour 3 litres from the 3-litre jug into the 5-litre jug.

Next state

	8-litre jug	5-litre jug	3-litre jug
Contents of the jugs:	3	5	0
Goal contents of the jugs:	4	4	0

Difference: 1   1 = 2

(B)Move possibility number two: Pour 2 litres from the 5-litre jug into the 8-litre jug.

Next state

	8-litre jug	5-litre jug	3-litre jug
Contents of the jugs:	5	0	3
Goal contents of the jugs:	4	4	0

Difference: 1   4 = 5

(C) Move possibility number three: Pour 3 litres from the 8-litre jug into the 5-litre jug.

Next state

	8-litre jug	5-litre jug	3-litre jug
Contents of the jugs:	0	5	3
Goal contents of the jugs:	4	4	0

Difference: 4   1 = 5

(D) Move possibility number four: Pour 3 litres from the 3-litre jug into the 8-litre jug.

Next state

	8-litre jug	5-litre jug	3-litre jug
Contents of the jugs	6	2	0
Goal contents of the jugs:	4	4	0

Difference: 2   2 = 4

Figure 1.17   Four move possibilities from state 3, 2, 3 of the 8, 5, 3 Waterjugs problem.

critical points in the problem. The alternatives, of course, lead solvers back to states near the start of the problem, which is where people would often find themselves if they used only means-ends analysis in solving the problem. This is because the problem cannot be solved without violating the means-ends strategy, that is unless the solver is willing to choose moves that lead (temporarily) away from the goal rather than choosing moves that *seem* to lead towards the goal. The usefulness of a strategy, then, is dependent in part on the underlying structure of the problem. Imagine having the goal of trying to find your way out of an unfamiliar building. You are on the second floor, and you know that the entrance to the building faces north. You find a stairway that faces south. Would you refuse to use the stairs?

People are able to solve the problem because they store a representation in long-term memory of the problem states that have been visited previously, and part of their strategy is to avoid states they recognize as old. In fact, once you enter the second state on either solution path, you could solve the problem by working out all possible moves and always choosing the move that leads to a new state of the problem. Unfortunately, the capacity of working memory limits the amount of information that can be held about successor states and as a result move selection may sometimes be based on incomplete information.

Activity 7

Work out the means-ends values for the record of moves you yourself made in solving the 8, 5, 3 problem, and then answer the following questions.

1 When (if) you found yourself in state 2, 5, 1 did you move forward on your next move (to state 7, 0, 1) or did you move to either state 0, 5, 3 or 3, 5, 0, both of which have lower means-ends values?

2 When (if) you found yourself at state 6, 2, 0 did you move forward on your next move or did you return to one of the four states at the top of Figure 1.16?

3 All together, how many times did you find yourself in one of the states at the top of the graph?

5.3   Polson's three-stage program

The computer model devised by Polson and his colleagues provides a close simulation of human behaviour on a number of Waterjug problems. The model incorporates a three-stage process of interactions between means-ends and memory processes. Information about problem states visited during the solution to the problem is stored in long-term memory. Because people sometimes fail to remember which states they have visited in the problem, the probability that the program will remember any state entered during the solution is set to .90. Working memory holds information about the current state of the problem, successor states, and state evaluation information. In the program, working memory is limited to holding information about three successor states at most. Because most states of the problem have four possible successors, some information may be lost from working memory during some stages of processing.

In stage 1, the program selects moves according to the following criteria. A move that would lead directly to the goal state is always taken. A move that leads back to the start state is never taken. Illegal moves are rejected. Otherwise, if a proposed move does not seem to lead too far away from the goal, and leads to a new state of the problem, the move is taken with a high probability. There is a smaller probability of a move leading to a previously visited state being selected.

In stage 2 the program generates successors in turn and selects the first move that would lead to a new problem state. If none of the successor states leads to a new state, stage 3 is entered.

In stage 3 the number of successor states determines how a move is chosen. If working memory is not overloaded, the best move of those available in working memory (that is, the move with the lowest means-ends value) is chosen. If working memory is overloaded (that is, if there are more than three successor states) the program randomly selects a move from the moves retained in working memory.

Polson and his associates have carried out numerous experimental tests of this model. As one example, in order to test the means-ends assumption, Atwood and Polson (1976) compared the behaviour of the program in solving four different problems, including the 8, 5, 3 problem and a Waterjugs problem with jugs holding 24, 21 and 3 litres. In this latter problem there are no states that violate the evaluation function, so the program does not experience any of the difficulties it experiences with the former problem. Atwood and Polson compared the number of moves required for both the computer program and groups of human subjects in solving the four different problems. They found an exceptionally high correspondence between the choice of moves made by the program and the observed behaviour of experimental subjects.

Atwood, Masson and Polson (1980) performed an experiment that provided a strong test of the 'no planning' hypothesis. They noted that the results of Atwood and Polson's experiment could be interpreted as meaning that heavy memory load was what prevented subjects from planning a sequence of moves, or setting up intermediate sub-goals. Reducing memory load might enable planning activities. In order to test the hypothesis, Atwood *et al.* presented one group of subjects with information about all the moves available from each state in the problem and the consequence of making any particular move. In this condition then, processing capacity was considerably extended by obviating the need for the subject to work out a sequence of moves. In a second condition processing resources were extended still further by providing subjects with even more information. As well as being told which moves were available from each state, and what states would result from making any move, subjects were provided with information on states they had already visited. If subjects were prevented from planning a sequence of moves only because they had trouble remembering which states they had been in before, then this condition should have removed the difficulty. In a control condition subjects were given none of this extra information.

Although the results showed that the more information provided, the fewer moves were required in finding a solution to the problem – compelling evidence that memory limitations play a central role in problem-solving situations – the improvement was far less than would be expected if subjects were able to plan a sequence of moves. Polson argues that the only kind of planning that occurs in this type of problem is a corollary of the insight that states near the initial state of the problem should be avoided. The plan then is simply to avoid those states when selecting a move.

The Polson model has been extended to account for behaviour on other transformation problems (Jeffries, Polson, Razran and Atwood, 1977; Polson and Jeffries, 1982) including the Towers of Hanoi and Missionaries and Cannibals problems. Polson and his associates have amassed a considerable catalogue of problem-solving performances on transformation problems, including the way people solve the same problem a second and third time. They have found, as we would expect, that with experience on the same problem, subjects get better at solving the problem, mainly as a result of changes in strategy between one presentation of a problem and the next. However, in line with other research presented in Section 3.3, they have also found that people have great difficulty transferring experience from one type of transformation problem to other, but closely related, types of problem.

SAQ 10
On the next page is a protocol which I took from an adult subject trying to solve the 8, 5, 3 Waterjug problem. The protocol contains the moves actually made by the subject and her comments while she worked on the problem. Before attempting to answer the questions below you might like to re-read the discussion on protocol analysis in Section 4.3.

(a) In your own words, what processes do you think are indicated by each individual phrase of the protocol? I have already labelled the first three phrases according to my own intuitions about the processes reflected by the statements.

(b) What is the means-ends value for the first three moves made by this subject?

Initial state

| Jug capacity | 8 5 3 |
| Jug contents | 8 0 0 |

Actual moves

First: Jug 8 = > Jug 3 = 5 0 3
Second: Jug 8 = > Jug 5 = 0 5 3

1 I'm not getting very far with this.
   [Meta-comment: the subject evaluates her own progress on the problem]
2 The five-litre jug and the three-litre jug are both full...
   [Rehearsal: the subject refreshes her memory about the current state of the problem]
3 so I can either pour the three litres into the eight-litre jug...
   [Move-generation: the subject considers a possible transformation of the current state]
4 or I could pour the five litres into the eight.
5 Well, I want the three-litre jug empty, don't I?
6 So, I want to pour out the three litres into the eight-litre jug.

   Third: Jug 3 = > Jug 8 = 3 5 0

7 That means I've got three litres in the eight-litre jug, and five litres in the five-litre jug.

Summary of Section 5

- People's ability to plan ahead on difficult transformation problems is limited by (1) the fact that they may have only a partial understanding of the underlying structure of the problem, and (2) memory limitations. The first limitation may preclude the setting of intermediate sub-goals and the second limitation prevents the planning of a sequence of moves.

- An important strategy people use in solving transformation problems involves selecting moves which bring them closer to the goal – means-ends analysis. Unfortunately, the solution to some problems involves temporary movement away from the goal.

- Polson's model of problem solving on transformation problems conjoins a modified form of means-ends analysis and a limited capacity working memory and long-term memory processes. Working memory holds information about the current state of the problem, successors to the current state and state evaluation information. The limitations of working memory affect move selection processes because of the loss of some information during processing.

6   *Conclusions*

Cognitive psychologists have gone a long way in developing a scientific basis for studying problem solving. Besides devising methods for classifying problems, they have provided a number of important tools for carrying out problem-solving research. State space analysis provides a tool for characterizing the underlying structure of well-defined problems having relatively small problem spaces, and comparing the structure of problems having different surface characteristics. Collecting and analysing verbal protocols provides us with invaluable (but problematic) data on ongoing solution processes. Computers have been influential in forcing psychologists to be completely explicit in formulating theories of problem solving, and in providing rigorous tests of such theories.

Early research showed that problem difficulty is a function of: the structure of a problem; characteristics of the human information processing system; previous experience; the strategy employed in solving a problem; and even the way the problem is presented. Problem solving was described as a search in problem spaces. Means-ends analysis was shown to be one powerful general method for guiding a search for solutions to transformation problems.

The toy-world problems that received most attention were very well defined and required little knowledge for their solution. Although a great deal was learned about problem solving on such problems, it had yet to be shown that the same methods could be used to analyse and understand problem solving in messier, real-world problem-solving situations. As a result, many researchers began to study problem solving in the more complex environments of high school and university classrooms. This part of the story will be taken up in Part III.

Much early research was concerned with the conditions under which transfer of learning occurred, or failed to occur. A recurrent and intriguing finding was that although people benefit from repeated experience with the same problem, they often have great difficulty in transferring learning from one problem to different, but closely related problems. Findings such as these led some psychologists to explore the nature of transfer processes. We shall discuss the beginnings of this research in Part II.

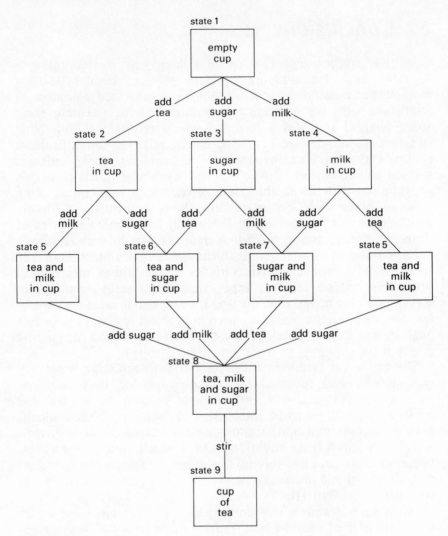

Answer to Activity 3

Part II
Analogical Problem
Solving

Contents

1   *Introduction*

A friend of mine has been keeping a catalogue of the events his young son understands through analogy. In one example, the child was watching his father cut the grass. The child said that it was like the grass getting a haircut. Of course, that is a nice way of understanding grass cutting, because the child would be able to think about grass cutting in terms of what he already knew about having his hair cut. For example, getting your hair cut can be itchy, irritating, and eventually boring, but your hair doesn't seem to suffer much – your hair doesn't hurt while it's being cut. Perhaps the grass doesn't feel anything either (although the ground might get 'irritated'). Maybe it just keeps growing back, like hair. What's underground? A limitless supply of grass? Does a head contain a limitless supply of hair that just keeps pushing its way out? What would happen if somebody cut your hair with a lawnmower, or the grass with a pair of scissors? Is there something beyond the *functional* similarity of the cutting implements that should be taken into consideration?

It could be argued, as Gentner and Gentner (1980) have pointed out, that people don't really use knowledge about one type of event (getting your hair cut) in *reasoning* about a different type of event (cutting the grass). It is possible that reasoning about an event such as cutting the grass occurs independently of any knowledge of analogous events, but that the analogous event provides a convenient framework for talking about the reasoning. That people actively use old knowledge in trying to understand new events or problems has been convincingly and elegantly shown in an experiment carried out by Gentner and Gentner (1980). The experiment involved two groups of subjects. One group was told that the flow of electricity could be understood in terms of the movement of crowds in a place like Euston station, and that a resistor was like a turnstile through which only one person could pass at a time. The other group was told that the flow of electricity could be understood in terms of the flow of water through pipes, and that a resistor could be thought of as a 'skinny' section of pipe, which produces a drop in water pressure. Gentner and Gentner presented the two groups of subjects with a problem in understanding the effect of a pair of resistors in the flow of electricity through a system. The voltage in an electrical system changes when a current passes through a resistor. The effect of a *pair* of resistors depends on the way in which the resistors are connected. If the resistors are connected in series, that is, one after the other, the total effect is a drop in voltage, by comparison with a single resistor. However, if resistors are connected in parallel, that is, side by side, then a greater current flow occurs than would occur given a single resistor. Gentner and Gentner argued that subjects given the water pipe analogy would predict that voltage would drop in all situations involving resistors, because they would think of resistors (skinny sections of pipe) as an impediment to water flow. They predicted that subjects given the moving crowds analogy should do better because they would think of two turnstiles (resistors) connected in parallel as facilitating the movement of people, while two turnstiles connected in series would slow people down more than a single turnstile would. The results showed that the answers given by the two groups of subjects could be predicted by the model of electricity flow they had previously been taught. These findings suggest that people do interpret a new problem in terms of what they know already. The general term for the use of problem strategies derived from experience with similar problems is *analogical problem solving*. The idea is that people solve problems by identifying analogies between old problems (hair cutting) and new problems (lawn mowing). This is another example of the *transfer* of past experience with one type of problem to another, for example, between the Towers of Hanoi and the Chinese Tea Ceremony problems.

Summary of Section 1

- People often understand and talk about events, including their own problem-solving behaviour, using their knowledge of analogous events as a framework.
- Gentner and Gentner have shown that people can also solve problems using knowledge of the strategies they would use to solve similar problems. This is known as analogical problem solving, and is an example of the transfer of problem-solving abilities or learning.

2   Analysing ill-defined problems

All of the research on the transfer of learning discussed in Part I was concerned with well-defined transformation problems (see Part I, Section 3.3) in which the initial and goal states and legal operators are clearly defined. This meant that identities between the solution to isomorphic problems (for example, Towers of Hanoi or the Chinese Tea Ceremony) and similarities between homomorphic problems (for example, Missionaries and Cannibals and Jealous Husbands) could be easily identified. In this section I will describe recent research on ill-defined problems where it is not clear what the problem is, much less the solution. Research on such problems brings the analysis of problem solving much closer to our everyday concerns, as many of the problems with which we are confronted are ill defined in some respect. An ill-defined problem is one that lacks clear details of the initial or goal states or which does not include a complete specification of the operators (moves) that can be employed in solving the problem.

Since you have not yet had an opportunity to analyse an ill-defined problem, I will begin by presenting you with details of what I will call the 'fortress' problem.

Activity 1

The *fortress problem* tells a story about a general who wanted to rid his country of a tyrant. You should read the story all the way through at least once, and then answer the SAQs that follow, referring back to the story as often as you want. It is very important for you to attempt both SAQs because the experience will make it a lot easier for you to follow the discussion in the following sections.

A small country fell under the iron rule of a dictator. The dictator ruled the country from a strong fortress. The fortress was situated in the middle of the country, surrounded by farms and villages. Many roads radiated outward from the fortress like the spokes on a wheel. A great general raised a large army at the border, vowing to capture the fortress and free the country of the dictator. The general knew that if his entire army could attack the fortress at once it could be captured. His troops were poised at the head of one of the roads leading to the fortress, ready to attack. However, a spy brought the general a disturbing report. The ruthless dictator had planted mines on each of the roads. The mines were set so that small bodies of men could pass over them safely, since the dictator needed to be able to move troops and workers to and from the fortress. However, any large force would detonate the mines. Not only would this blow up the road and render it impassable, but the dictator would then destroy many villages in retaliation. A full-scale direct attack on the fortress therefore appeared impossible.

The general, however, was undaunted. He divided his army up into small groups and dispatched each group to the head of a different road. When all was ready he gave the signal, and each group charged down a different road. All of the small groups passed safely over the mines, and the army then attacked the fortress in full strength. In this way, the general was able to capture the fortress and overthrow the dictator.

SAQ 11
Referring back to the text of the fortress problem, fill in the details for each of the following. *Hint*: The first paragraph of the fortress problem story contains the details of the problem, and the second paragraph contains the solution. So all the information you need to answer this SAQ is contained in the first paragraph.

Initial state:

Goal state:

Operators:

Operator restrictions:

SAQ 12
In what sense is the fortress problem ill defined?

2.1   Duncker's 'radiation' problem

In early studies of problem solving on 'practical problems', Duncker, the famous Gestalt psychologist, made extensive use of the *radiation problem*. Duncker was a very early exponent of verbal protocols. In his experiments (Duncker, 1945) he asked his subjects to read the radiation problem and then to try to think of as many solutions to the problem as they could. They were encouraged to use pencil and paper to draw figures or make any notes they wished, and were asked to speak aloud anything at all that came into their minds.

Activity 2
Try to solve the radiation problem before reading further. Get some paper and a pencil and write down as many possible solutions as you can think of. Even if you can immediately think of reasons why a possible solution should be rejected, write it down. Spend at least five minutes solving it.

Suppose you are a doctor faced with a patient who has a malignant tumour in his stomach. It is impossible to operate on the patient, but unless the tumour is destroyed the patient will die. There is a kind of ray that can be used to destroy the tumour. If the rays reach the tumour all at once with sufficiently high intensity, the tumour will be destroyed. Unfortunately at this intensity the healthy tissue that the rays pass through on the way to the tumour will also be destroyed. At lower intensities the rays are harmless to healthy tissue, but they will not affect the tumour either. What type of procedure might be used to destroy the tumour with the rays, and at the same time avoid destroying the healthy tissues?

SAQ 13
Using the text of the radiation problem, specify each of the following:

Initial state:

Goal state:

Operators:

Operator restrictions:

SAQ 14
In what sense is the radiation problem ill defined? Now try to think of other possible solutions to the radiation problem.

The initial and goal states in the radiation problem are well defined, as are the restrictions on the use of any operators that might be used to solve the problem. The operator restrictions disallow surgery or any physical action that would destroy healthy tissue. Nevertheless, the problem as a whole is ill defined because the possible operators are specified only very generally: *use rays* to destroy the tumour. In order to solve the problem an operator must be transformed into something a lot more specific, that is, *how* to use the rays to destroy the tumour without destroying healthy tissues.

One way you yourself might have solved the radiation problem was to use what you knew about the solution to the fortress problem as a framework for thinking about how to use the special rays to destroy the patient's stomach tumour. This solution involves 'dividing the rays' and directing numerous applications of low intensity rays at the tumour simultaneously – analogous to the general's solution which involved dividing an army and sending numerous small units along the many roads radiating out from the fortress. If you did this, you solved the tumour problem by applying an analogy from the fortress problem. In fact, you have just taken part in an informal experiment; an experiment similar in spirit to an experiment performed by Gick and Holyoak to investigate analogical problem solving.

2.2   *Gick and Holyoak's experiments*

In this section I will describe two of the many experiments conducted by Gick and Holyoak. In Experiment 1, Gick and Holyoak investigated subjects' ability to solve problems by analogy when they were given a hint to do so, and in Experiment 3 they investigated subjects' ability to notice spontaneously an analogy. The details of these experiments are presented in Techniques Boxes B and C.

TECHNIQUES BOX B

Gick and Holyoak (1980)
Experiment 1

Rationale

Gick and Holyoak set out to discover whether subjects could use analogies in solving the radiation problem if they were given a hint to do so. The experimenters devised a number of story analogies that differed in the type of solution suggested. Gick and Holyoak predicted that subjects would be significantly influenced by the type of solution presented in the particular story analogy they were asked to read before solving the radiation problem.

Method

Gick and Holyoak informed their subjects that the experiment was in two parts. One group (the control group) was simply asked to solve the radiation problem. For the three experimental groups, the first part of the experiment was presented as a memory recall task, in which subjects would be presented with a *story* (actually, a version of the fortress problem), and their task would be to summarize the story. All of the story analogies contained exactly the same first paragraph (the first paragraph of the fortress story presented in Activity 1), but differed according to the solution presented in the second paragraph. In one version (called the Tunnel story) the general dug a tunnel to the fort. In another version (called the Open Supply Route story), the general used one of the main roads to the fortress, which he knew the tyrant kept open as a supply route. The third version was called the Attack-Dispersion story, and contained the convergence solution with which you are familiar from Activity 1.

The subjects were informed that the second part of the experiment involved a problem-solving task. In this part of the experiment they would be presented with a problem and asked to report as many possible solutions as they could think of. The subjects were told that in solving the radiation problem they should try to use the story problem they had already read and summarized. They were allowed to re-read the story analogy whenever they wished. Subjects were asked to provide 'think aloud' verbal protocols as they were solving the problem.

Results

All subjects who had been given the Attack-Dispersion solution to the fortress problem proposed a dispersion solution to the radiation problem. This solution was proposed by only ten per cent of the subjects who had received the Open Supply Route story, twenty per cent of subjects who had received the Tunnel story, and none of the control subjects. Seventy per cent of subjects who had been given the Open

Supply Route story proposed 'open passage' solutions (for example, sending high-intensity rays down the oesophagus), significantly many more than any of the other groups. Eighty per cent of subjects who had received the Tunnel story suggested operating on the patient.

TECHNIQUES BOX C

Gick and Holyoak (1980)
Experiment 3

Rationale

This experiment was designed to investigate the effects of processing requirements in more realistic conditions than those in which previous experiments had been conducted. In everyday situations, people may not be given a hint to use an analogy in solving a problem. Also, when solving problems by analogy people have to search memory for a relevant analog problem.

Method

As in Experiment 1, subjects were told that the first part of the experiment involved a memory recall task and the second part involved a problem-solving task. Two groups of subjects were presented with the fortress problem story that contained the Attack-Dispersion solution, plus two other stories that were completely disanalogous to the radiation problem. The fortress problem story was the second story presented to all groups. Subjects were asked to read the stories and to recall them in as much detail as possible. Both groups were then asked to find as many solutions as they could to the radiation problem. The only difference between the two groups was that one group was given the following hint: 'In solving this problem you may find that one of the stories you read before will give you a hint for a solution of this problem'. The other group received no hint.

Results

Ninety-two per cent of subjects in the hint condition proposed the dispersion solution to the radiation problem, whereas only twenty per cent of the subjects in the no hint condition proposed this solution.

The results of Experiment 1 showed that subjects were very good at employing an analogy when they were told to do so. The results also showed that the nature of the prior analog story had a significant determining effect on the kind of solution that was proposed for the radiation problem. In all conditions, the most frequent solution was that suggested by the story analogy that subjects had been given in the first part of the experiment.

In the 'no hint' condition of Experiment 3, Gick and Holyoak were trying to lead their subjects to believe that the two parts of the experiment were unrelated so that they could investigate whether or not subjects would recognize spontaneously that information acquired in the first part was relevant to the problem presented in the second part of the experiment.

When I introduced you to the fortress problem I presented it under the pretext of giving you a chance to analyse an ill-defined problem, but my real purpose was to give you an opportunity to experience for yourself the kind of situation Gick and Holyoak's subjects faced. I don't know whether or not you perceived the relationship between the fortress and radiation problems, but Gick and Holyoak's results showed that subjects were quite good at employing knowledge of the fortress problem and its solution when solving the radiation problem *only* if the experimenter gave them a hint that the problems were related. If subjects were not given a hint − as was the case in my informal experiment − the analogy was not so helpful.

SAQ 15
In Section 3.3 of Part I I discussed research by Reed *et al.* on transfer between the Missionaries and Cannibals and Jealous Husbands problems. How are Gick and Holyoak's findings related to the findings of Reed *et al.*?

In another experiment, Gick and Holyoak presented the fortress story *after* subjects had already begun work on the radiation problem. In this experiment subjects were informed that the experimenters were interested in 'incubation' phenomena (that is, the effects of taking time off from solution attempts and doing a different task for a while). The subjects were asked to work on a problem (the radiation problem) for a period of time, after which they would be given the fortress story to read as a filler task. Even in this condition most subjects still failed to recognize the fortress story as analogous to the radiation problem unless they were given a hint. I tried to replicate the 'hint' condition of Gick and Holyoak's experiments by asking you to think about the problem again after you had answered SAQs 11−14, the answers to which were intended to demonstrate the similarities between the two problems.

If it seems incredible to you that Gick and Holyoak's subjects failed to notice the analogy between the fortress and radiation problems, even when the fortress problem was introduced while subjects were attempting to solve the radiation problem, consider the following situation. Imagine that you are a student taking two different types of course during a certain academic year; for the sake of argument, Philosophy and Introductory Psychology. At the end of the year, it turns out that both of your examinations are to be held on the same day. You sit your Philosophy examination in the morning and the Psychology examination in the afternoon. (You do not need to have taken a course in either subject in order to follow the point I want to make.) During the Philosophy examination you answer the following question:

> If asked to describe 'reality', would you base your description on existentialist or realist philosophy? Justify your choice.

In the afternoon, you find the following among the questions on the Introductory Psychology examination paper:

> If you knew someone who needed treatment for a neurotic condition, would you recommend behaviour modification or psychoanalysis? Why?

Now imagine that you consider answering this question. But you start daydreaming a bit, thinking about the Philosophy examination, wondering how well you performed, even briefly reviewing your answers to the questions you attempted. Do you think you would have seen a connection between your current problem and your answer to the question about the nature of reality?

You could be forgiven for thinking that these examination questions are unrelated, that your answer to the Philosophy question would not help you in answering the Psychology question. But, in fact, both questions are of a *type* in which the examinee is being asked to compare and contrast, and to evaluate, different ideas on the one hand, and treatment methods on the other. If you had devoted a lot of time to organizing an answer to a question of this type on the Philosophy paper, then the organization of the answer might well serve as a framework for answering the question on the Psychology paper. The subjects in Gick and Holyoak's experiments, where the fortress story was presented in the context of a 'memory recall task' and the radiation story in the context of a 'problem-solving task', were in much the same situation as a person sitting examinations in unrelated fields. In both situations, it is exceedingly difficult to perceive the connection between events where the relationship is buried under a lot of surface dissimilarities.

Summary of Section 2

- In this section you were presented with two ill-defined problems: the first was accompanied by its solution, and you were asked to solve the second. The solution involved transforming a quite general specification of operators into specific actions that could be performed to achieve the goal of the second problem.
- Gick and Holyoak have carried out a series of experiments investigating the solving of an ill-defined problem, where an analogical problem and solution were also presented. They repeatedly found that the vast majority of their subjects used the analogy to solve the current problem only when they were given a hint that the two problems were related.
- Gick and Holyoak also found that the vast majority of subjects could successfully use the solution to a previous problem in solving an analogous problem once they were given a hint to do so.

3 Problem representations in memory

Gick and Holyoak suggest that analogical problem solving is an especially useful heuristic in situations that people find somewhat novel. The radiation problem is novel for most people because they know very little about medical procedures or about 'rays' or about whether 'rays' can be 'divided'. Faced with such a problem, a very useful strategy would involve searching memory for an analogous situation. If an analogous situation were found, then the solution to that previous situation might serve as a framework for thinking about a solution to the current problem.

A prerequisite of analogical problem solving is that there should be a mental representation in memory of an analogous problem. Gick and Holyoak, borrowing terms from Gentner (1979), call the previously experienced problem the *base problem* and the current problem the *target problem*. One of the important issues in analogical problem-solving research is to understand how the description of the current target problem is used in searching long-term memory for a base problem. It is assumed that the target problem is represented in short-term *working memory* and the analogous *base problem* is represented in *long-term memory*. The problem, then, becomes one of *memory retrieval*; in other words, the retrieval of a problem which is analogous to the current problem. If a person succeeds in retrieving an analogous problem from long-term memory, for example the fortress problem, this will result in positive transfer to the new problem; if not, the new problem, for example, the radiation problem, will have to be tackled from scratch. (It is also possible for an old problem solution to be retrieved which is in fact a *false analogy*. False analogies can lead to incorrect solutions, for example, assuming that because you have met one ferocious red-headed person, all redhaired people are quick tempered, leading to an inappropriate solution to the problem of reacting to redheaded strangers.)

To see why finding a good analogy is a difficult matter, compare the representations of the fortress and radiation problems, which were given in the answers to SAQs 11 and 13, and which are also presented in Figure 2.1.

(a) Long-term memory
    Base problem (fortress)

INITIAL STATE: General outside fortress with army. Tyrant inside fortress. Roads radiating out from the fortress have been mined. Large bodies of men passing along a road would set off the mines, destroying the roads and making them impassable. If the roads are destroyed, the tyrant would destroy many villages in retaliation.

GOAL: General overthrows tyrant.

OPERATORS: General can use army to attack fortress.

RESTRICTIONS: General must avoid destruction of army and villages.

SOLUTION: General divides army into small units. General sends units down the many roads radiating out from the fortress. General reassembles army at fortress. Army attacks fortress in strength.

(b) Working memory
    Target problem (radiation)

INITIAL STATE: Tumour in patient's stomach. Doctor is not allowed to operate. Doctor has special ray which can be used for treatment. High intensity rays destroy healthy tissues as well as tumours. Low intensity rays neither destroy tumours nor damage healthy tissues.

GOAL: Doctor destroys tumour.

OPERATORS: Doctor can use special rays to destroy tumour.

RESTRICTIONS: Doctor must avoid damage to healthy tissue.

SOLUTION: ?????

Figure 2.1

The striking thing about these representations is that they have nothing in common 'on the surface'. In the one case, the objects represented are things such as a hospital patient, a doctor, special rays, and so forth. In the other, the objects are a dictator and a general, armies, mines, roads and villages. So there is a difficulty in explaining how the mind is able to find correspondences between events which are, on the face of it, completely unrelated. An interesting feature of Gick and Holyoak's findings is that, while the majority of their subjects failed to notice spontaneously the analogy, a significant minority did notice it. Why does the majority fail?

3.1 Levels of abstraction

Gick and Holyoak make the point that stories or problems can be represented at many different levels of abstraction. At a surface level of abstraction the fortress and radiation stories would contain the different details actually presented in the stories. At a deeper level of abstraction, though, both stories could be described in terms of someone having the *goal* of 'overcoming an obstacle'. Since there are few – if any – correspondences between the two problems at the surface level of description (generals and doctors, and so on), Gick and Holyoak argue that the process of being reminded of one problem in the presence of the other must be mediated through deep-level abstractions of the two problems which reveal their similarities.

Kintsch and Van Dijk (1978) proposed a theory of how memory representations are structured in long-term memory. They suggested that *memory structures* are constructed from experience as a result of abstracting out the essential content, or 'gist' of a situation. Kintsch and Van Dijk have proposed a number of processes for constructing abstract representations of the events we hear or read about, including deletion, generalization and construction. In order to see how these processes are thought to work, consider the first three lines of the fortress story:

> A small country fell under the iron rule of a dictator. The dictator ruled the country from a strong fortress. The fortress was situated in the middle of the country.

A concrete surface representation of this story would contain most of the details of the story. A slightly more abstract representation could be created by the *deletion process* which removes inessential details from the surface-level description. Deletion reduces the amount of information in the structure of a memory representation, but preserves the 'gist' of the story. Applied to the first three lines of the fortress story, deletion would result in the following representation.

> A country was ruled by a dictator. The dictator ruled from a fortress in the middle of the country.

Even more abstract levels of representation could be achieved by making successive deletions. If the deletion process were applied again, this time to the second-level abstraction, we might have:

> A fortress was located in the centre of the country.

The *generalization process* also reduces the amount of information in a memory structure. An example of generalization would be the transformation of a great deal of detailed information in the text about the 'planting of mines' and 'resultant danger to troops and villages' and 'the general's plan of attack' into a more abstract description such as: 'the general wanted to prevent widespread destruction'.

The *construction process* adds information rather than reduces it. Construction involves making inferences about events and motivations which are implied rather than stated directly. In psychology inferences are often defined as 'going beyond' what is actually present in a story or problem situation. Understanding often involves the ability to attribute causes to the actions people perform. For example, nowhere in the fortress story is it directly stated that the *reason* the tyrant planted mines in the roads was to prevent an attack on his fortress by a large army. Nor does the story state why the general divided his army and sent small units down all the roads converging on the fortress. But most people automatically infer that his reasons were that he did not want to have his army destroyed and he did want to protect the villages. Construction processes often involve adding information to a representation in terms of inferred *causal relations*, that is, the goals that can be attributed to actors in order to explain sequences of actions.

SAQ 16
Here are two little stories.
1 Debbie told Judy that John was back in London. That night, Judy moved to Sheffield.
2 As George rounded the corner he saw a police car sitting in front of his house. He did an about-turn and quickly walked away.
   (a) What would you say is the common causal relation between the pair of events described in the two different stories? *Hint*: What goal is shared by Judy and George?
   (b) On a scale from 1 to 10, how similar are these two stories 'on the surface'?
   (c) On a scale from 1 to 10, how similar are these two stories in terms of the causal relation you identified in (a)?

When causal relations are made explicit, the similarities between seemingly different events become somewhat more transparent. A memory retrieval search would have less difficulty matching abstract descriptions that reveal similarities between two representations than it would have matching the surface-level representations involving the specific details of the two problems. However, one major difficulty with hypothesizing 'abstraction processes' like Kintsch and Van Dijk's is that at the deepest level of abstraction all problems might seem to be analogous. For instance, at the deepest level of abstraction, the radiation and fortress problems could both be described as follows: *somebody did something to achieve something*.

This same description would also apply to a story about somebody stealing a car to get to an appointment on time, or to any other story about someone performing some act in order to achieve some goal, although those analogies would not be helpful. Perception of the relationship between two representations depends upon the level of abstraction at which they are matched. At intermediate levels, many similarities will be apparent, but not all of the irrelevant differences will have been abstracted. Gick and Holyoak argue that the optimal level is that at which the similarities between two representations are maximized, and differences minimized. This optimum level would correspond to an intermediate stage of abstraction.

The importance of research into memory retrieval processes for understanding problem-solving behaviour is highlighted by Gick and Holyoak's findings: that subjects often fail to notice spontaneously the relationship between a current problem and stored knowledge. Advances in our understanding of memory storage and retrieval processes would do a lot to enhance our understanding of analogical transfer of solutions between problems.

Summary of Section 3

- In analogical problem solving the current target problem, as it is represented in short-term working memory, is used to retrieve a representation of a previously experienced base problem from long-term memory.
- Gick and Holyoak suggest that for a helpful analogy to be retrieved, the target and base problems must be represented at an appropriate level of abstraction. While there may be few correspondences between surface level details of two different problems, deeper-level abstractions may reveal similarities.
- Kintsch and Van Dijk propose that concrete representations of events are made more abstract by three types of process: deletion of inessential details; generalization, by substituting the general categories to which events belong; and construction, by adding inferences, including causal relations.
- If abstraction processes are taken to the deepest level then all problems are analogous. Gick and Holyoak argue that the optimal level of abstraction is an intermediate one where similarities are maximized and differences are minimized.

4 Applying solutions

So far we have been talking about how problems are represented in memory in a way that allows a new problem to be analysed and recognized as similar or different. But naturally the purpose of all this is that the solutions to earlier problems can be used to help the problem solver to adapt them to solve the new problem. In the problem representations given in Figure 2.1, the representation of the fortress problem contains 'solution' information. But the problem is how the solution to this problem can be transformed into a solution for the analogous radiation problem. Assuming that a person has recognized that the fortress and radiation problems are related (through being given a hint, say), we would still be faced with the problem of how the solution to the fortress problem (dividing and reassembling an army) could be translated into a solution to the radiation problem (convergence of low intensity rays directed at the tumour from a number of different sources).

Duncker (1945) suggested that problem solving involved both problem solution processes and problem reformulation processes in turns. According to this theory, a person would solve, or partially solve, one part of a problem and then use the solution as a means of refining what the problem is. With this new, somewhat clearer perspective on the problem, problem solving would again be initiated. Gick and Holyoak investigated their subjects' strategies in solving the radiation problem by evaluating their verbal protocols. Like Duncker, they found that some subjects arrived at a solution only after trying out and rejecting or modifying partial solutions. They called this process of refining solutions *solution development*.

4.1 Solution development

In order to demonstrate the process of a gradual development of a solution, consider the progress of one of Gick and Holyoak's subjects, called S15 (subject number 15). S15 had been presented with the fortress story before attempting the radiation problem. Relevant extracts from the subject's verbal protocol as she was trying to solve the radiation problem are presented in Table 2.1. The single comment made by the experimenter is preceded by 'E:' in the table.

I have divided the protocol into seven different segments, labelled (a), (b), (c), (d), (e), (f) and (X), in order to make my discussion easier to follow. Altogether S15 generated three possible solutions to the problem – in the segments marked (a), (b) and (d) in Table 2.1.

Table 2.1   Extract from protocol of S15 in Gick and Holyoak's experiment

Subject reads radiation problem.

(a) 'Alright I, what I most, what I'd probably do is send the ray at sufficiently high intensity and then take the risk that the tissues, the healthy tissues that would be destroyed, could be repaired later on.'

(b) 'Trying to relate this to the other problem, I could say that you could give multiple treatments of low-intensity ray. But from this problem it seems that they won't have an effect on the tumour... So I don't think that would work.'

Later...

(c) 'Alright, in that way my first suggestion would probably not be the way to go at it. Because that way you're getting low intensity so it won't destroy the tissue and hopefully over a period of time the additive effect of low intensity rays would kill the tumour. But from reading the article, I don't know if that would work or not, because it says that a low intensity ray doesn't have any effect on the tumour at all. So I don't know. I don't know any other possible ways of doing it.'

(X) *E: 'Would it help to possibly go back to the story and see whether you can apply that?'*

(d) 'Well, that's what I was trying to do here. It says here he divides his army into different small groups. Okay,... possibly. What they could do, but this is a whole new solution now, possibly what they could do is attack the tumour from a multiple of directions, with low intensity rays...

(e) and then, since you're coming in from all different directions ... with small intensity rays you're not going to be destroying the healthy tissue but...

(f) they'll all converge at the point of the tumour which will hopefully destroy the tumour.'

S15's first solution was simply to blast the tumour with high intensity rays and to repair any damage done to healthy tissues later. S15 announced her second proposed solution, (b), immediately after presenting this first solution. I presume that S15 realized that her first solution was not acceptable under the rules of the problem.

S15's second solution involved the application of a succession of low intensity rays to the tumour. Unfortunately, the protocol contains no information to indicate where these ideas came from. However, this solution has important elements (for example, weak rays) of the third solution, and as such appears to be an intermediate step towards the next and last solution. S15's reason for rejecting her second solution is that weak rays applied over time would not accumulate sufficient intensity to destroy the tumour. S15 arrived at the 'dispersion' solution of sending many weak rays simultaneously, (d), after prompting by the experimenter. At (e) and (f) the subject evaluates the solution with respect to the operator restrictions ('with small intensity rays you're not going to be destroying the healthy tissue') and the goal state ('they'll all converge at the point of the tumour which will hopefully destroy the tumour').

Activity 3
Re-read the protocol segments marked (X) and (d) in Table 2.1. What evidence is there that subject S15 relied on an abstract stored representation of the fortress story as a framework for thinking about and solving the radiation problem?

In fact, the protocol evidence indicates that S15 is not relying on a stored representation of the fortress problem at all, but is actually working out her solution by referring directly to the text of the fortress problem. Remember, though, that the point of the analysis is to try to gain some insight into the way analogical problem solving *might* work, given that we have no information to work with when people 'automatically' generate an analogous solution to a problem.

Protocol evidence such as we have been discussing adds plausibility to Gick and Holyoak's suggestion that analogical problem solving involves the construction of a series of solutions, each of which is an outgrowth of the previous solution. Moreover, each partial solution to a problem can serve as a retrieval cue for related information in memory. When related information is retrieved, it can be used as a framework in which to modify the most recent solution. The result would be a somewhat transformed solution that, in its turn, would serve as the next retrieval cue, and so on.

4.2 Acquisition of problem schemas

Although Gick and Holyoak have shown that people are capable of using previous knowledge in solving a current, related problem, their research also suggests that difficulty in locating relevant stored knowledge about solutions is an important obstacle to the use of analogical problem solving. Since people cannot rely on others to be always on hand to point out to them which problems are related, the evidence suggests that analogical problem solving is not a very useful heuristic in problem solving.

However, in the real world we are quite often provided with hints about how problems are related. Consider, for example, how students learn from scientific texts, such as physics, mathematics or computer programming. Such texts often present a few pages of material on a particular principle, plus a number of worked-out problems that illustrate the principle. At the end of the section a number of exercise problems are presented. The mere fact that a number of exercise problems are presented together can be regarded as a strong hint that the problems are somehow related, even though the surface characteristics of the problems may differ considerably. The purpose of presenting a number of related problems is to give students practice in solving problems of a particular type, and an opportunity to abstract the common properties among the different problems. The hope is that students will end up by storing in their memories a generalized abstraction which represents a general strategy for dealing with a whole class of problems. General strategies of this kind can be thought of as *schemas* for dealing with problems. *Problem-solving schemas* are memory representations which embody knowledge based on past experiences with a particular type of problem. The process of constructing such a representation is also called *schema learning*.

Gick and Holyoak (1983) conducted a series of experiments to investigate the conditions under which schema learning is most likely to occur. In some of these experiments Gick and Holyoak measured the effects of teaching a schema for 'convergence problems' more or less directly. For example, in one experiment they presented a group of subjects with a prior story analog, such as the fortress problem, plus a statement of the abstract principle underlying the solution to 'convergence problems': 'If you need a large force to accomplish some purpose, but are prevented from applying such a force directly, many smaller forces applied simultaneously from different directions may work just as well'. In a second condition, only the abstract principle was given before the radiation problem. In a third condition, the fortress problem alone was presented before the radiation problem. When Gick and Holyoak compared the number of analogous solutions in all conditions, both before and after a hint was given, they found that presenting an explicit statement of important aspects of the schema for convergence problems was no help at all. In fact, there was no difference in performance among the different conditions either before or after the hint. Upon reflection, these results should not seem very surprising – imagine trying to teach your neighbours about transformation problems using the Towers of Hanoi puzzle as the only example problem. Even if you added the principle, 'look for intermediate sub-goals while you work on the problem', you probably wouldn't be surprised if your neighbours weren't very good at recognizing other transformation problems.

Gick and Holyoak found that subjects were far more likely to acquire a problem schema if two prior analog stories were presented, instead of just one. For example, subjects were presented with both the fortress problem and a story about a fire at an oil rig. The firefighters had a vast quantity of fire retardant foam at their disposal, but they did not have a hose large enough to put a large quantity of foam on the fire quickly. The solution (you've guessed it) involved stationing a number of firefighters around the oil rig with all the small hoses that were available. Subjects were asked to read and summarize each story, and also to compare and contrast the stories, which they were allowed to re-read as and when they wanted. In this situation subjects were about twice as likely to generate an analogous solution to the radiation problem as a group of subjects who were asked to compare and contrast either the fortress problem or the firefighting problem with a second, non-analogous story. In another experiment, Gick and Holyoak found even larger transfer effects when subjects were provided with two prior analog stories plus a statement of the solution principle common to both.

The importance of problem schemas has been convincingly shown in a series of experiments conducted by Chi, Feltovich and Glaser (1981). In one of these experiments, Chi *et al.* asked PhD students (experts) and undergraduate students (novices) in physics to group twenty-four problems from a standard undergraduate physics text-book into categories, based on similarities in the way the problems should be solved. Interestingly, the experts took slightly (but not significantly) longer than the novices to sort the problems into categories, but both groups produced about eight or nine different problem categories altogether. The two groups did differ in terms of the problems they thought should be grouped together. The experts classified problems on the basis of fundamental laws of physics, such as Newton's first law. Novices, on the other hand, grouped problems on the basis of 'surface' features of the problems. For example, novices were likely to categorize two problems as members of the same class if the diagrams accompanying the problems both showed blocks on an inclined plane. In fact, the novices tended to call such problems 'inclined plane' problems. The experts, however, were able to distinguish between different types of problems that had surface similarities; rather, they grouped problems in terms of deep solution principles, such as 'Conservation of energy'.

Chi *et al.* concluded that experts' problem-solving schemas contain knowledge that enables them to classify problems in terms of the solution principles that should be used to solve particular types of problems.

According to Gick and Holyoak, recognition, or retrieval, of an analogous problem solution is the major difficulty solvers have to overcome in problem solving by analogy. In the numerous experiments reported by Gick and Holyoak, about eighty per cent of subjects succeeded in producing analogous solutions to the radiation problem when they were given a hint to use a prior story analog. This figure suggests that most people have little trouble with the solution application process once an analogy is noticed. Unfortunately, however, recent research by Reed, Dempster and Ettinger (1985) shows that things are not that simple.

Reed, Dempster and Ettinger point out that a single problem category may contain different types of problem. They argue that the usefulness of analogy in such domains should depend upon how similar a problem is to a previous problem for which a solution is already known. In algebra, for example, there is a category of problems known as 'distance problems'. Table 2.2 contains three different distance problems which were used in experiments by Reed, Dempster and Ettinger. Also presented in Table 2.2 are the equations appropriate for each of the three problems (don't worry about the details if you are unfamiliar with algebra problems). Problems 1 and 2 can both be solved using the same equation (but with different values for variables such as speed). Since the same equation can be

Table 2.2

Problem 1 (Practice problem):	Problem 2 (Equivalent problem):	Problem 3 (Similar problem):
A car travelling at a speed of 30 mph left a certain place at 10 am. At 11.30 am, another car departed from the same place at 40 mph and travelled the same route. In how many hours will the second car overtake the first car?	A car travels south at the rate of 30 mph. Two hours later, a second car leaves to overtake the first car using the same route and going at 45 mph. In how many hours will the second car overtake the first car?	A car leaves 3 hours after a large delivery truck but overtakes it by travelling 15 mph faster. If it takes the car 7 hours to reach the delivery truck, find the rate of each vehicle.
Solution equation: $30t = 40(t - 1.5)$	Solution equation: $30t = 45(t - 2)$	Solution equation: $10r = 7(r + 15)$

used to solve both problems, Reed, Dempster and Ettinger refer to such problems as 'equivalent' problems. Problem 3 is also a distance problem, but its solution involves a slight modification to the equation that solves Problems 1 and 2 (the minus sign inside the brackets must be changed to a plus sign). Reed, Dempster and Ettinger refer to problems that belonged to the same category but were of different types as 'similar' problems.

In one experiment, Reed *et al.* presented one group of subjects with a practice problem (for example, Problem 1 in Table 2.2) followed by an equivalent problem and then a related problem (for example, Problems 2 and 3, respectively, in Table 2.2). Another group of subjects was given a practice problem that was not related to the two target problems. In all cases, after the subjects had solved, or attempted to solve the practice problem, and before they were presented with the two target problems, the experimenters showed the subjects the correct solution equation for the practice problem they had been given. Subjects who were given a related practice problem, and solution, were told that the solution should help them solve the two target problems. Nothing was said about the relationship between the practice problem and the target problems to the subjects who were given the unrelated practice problem.

The results were extremely interesting. Initially there appeared to be no difference at all between the groups in the number of correct solutions to the target problems. This suggested that solving a related problem (and being shown a correct solution) did not help in solving either equivalent or similar problems. However, when Reed *et al.* compared the number of correct solution equations generated by the two different groups they did find a significant difference. The subjects who had been given a related practice problem were far more likely to at least use the correct equation in solving the target problems – but they still had trouble with the equations themselves, as shown by the fact that the overall number of solutions between the two groups did not differ. In a follow-up experiment, Reed *et al.* showed that memory for solutions is an important limiting factor on performance. In this experiment, two groups of subjects were given related practice problems only, plus two equivalent and similar target problems, but one group was allowed to keep the solution to the practice problem in view while they worked on the target problems, while the other group worked on the target problems only after the solution to the practice problem had been removed. Subjects who were allowed to consult the solution to the practice problem produced significantly more correct solutions to the equivalent target problem. Having the solution in view did not help with similar problems.

The most dramatic improvement in performance on equivalent problems occurred when Reed *et al.* presented subjects with elaborated solutions and allowed the subjects to refer to the solutions while they worked on target problems. Elaboration of the solution also produced considerable transfer even if subjects were not allowed to refer to the solution while working on the target problems, by comparison with a group of subjects who did not receive an elaborated solution, but considerably less than that produced by the group who were allowed to view the solution in the second part of the experiment. Interestingly, even elaboration did not result in transfer on similar problems. Table 2.3 contains a practice distance problem plus an elaborated solution.

The only condition in which subjects showed transfer from a practice problem to a similar problem occurred when Reed, Dempster and Ettinger presented practice problems which were either slightly more complex than a related, similar target problem, or when the practice and similar target problems were of equal complexity.

Table 2.3

A car travelling at a speed of 30 mph left a certain place at 10 am. At 11.30 am, another car departed from the same place at 40 mph and travelled the same route. In how many hours will the second car overtake the first car?

Answer: The problem is a distance-rate-time problem in which

distance $=$ rate $\times$ time

We begin by constructing a table to represent the distance, rate and time for each of the two cars. We want to find how long the second car travels before it overtakes the first car. We let 't' represent the number that we want to find and enter it into the table. The first car then travels $t + \frac{3}{2}$ hr because it left $1\frac{1}{2}$ hours earlier. The rates are 30 mph for the first car and 40 mph for the second car. Notice that the first car must travel at a slower rate if the second car overtakes it. We can now represent the distance each car travels by multiplying the rate and the time for each car. These values are shown in the table at the right.

Car	Distance (miles)	Rate (mph)	Time (hr)
First	$30(t + \frac{3}{2})$	30	$t + \frac{3}{2}$
Second	$40 \times t$	40	t

Because both cars have travelled the same distance when the second car overtakes the first, we set the two distances equal to each other:

$$60(t + \tfrac{3}{2}) = 40t$$

Solving for 't' yields the following:

$$30t + 45 = 40t$$
$$45 = 10t$$
$$t = 4.5 \text{ hr}$$

Because recent research into students' learning in geometry (Anderson, Greeno, Kline and Neves, 1981) and computer programming (Anderson, Farrell and Sauers, 1984) has shown that students rely heavily on worked-out examples (analogies) in solving exercise problems, the results of Reed, Dempster and Ettinger's research have important pedagogical implications. In short, their results suggest that considerable care should be taken in selecting practice problems that are closely related to the example problems used in texts. Solutions to example problems should be available to students, and the principle underlying the solution to a problem should be stated explicitly.

Summary of Section 4

- Once an analogy has been recognized and a base problem retrieved from memory, the solution of the base problem must be translated into a solution to the target problem.
- Gick and Holyoak have found that in analogical problem solving subjects may generate and develop a series of partial solutions to the target problem, a process they term solution development. They suggest that each successive partial solution serves as a retrieval cue for related information which then serves as a framework for modifying the most recent partial solution to produce a new one.
- Gick and Holyoak's experiments suggest that analogical problem solving may not be a useful heuristic in problem solving since the difficulty of analogous problems is often only overcome when a hint is given by the experimenter. However, hints are often more readily available for real-world problems.
- Experience of a number of related problems can result in the acquisition of a problem-solving schema, a general strategy for dealing with a particular type of problem. This process is called schema learning.
- Investigating schema learning, Gick and Holyoak found no difference in the number of analogical solutions produced by groups of subjects receiving one prior analog, or a statement of the abstract solution principle, or both. However, subjects were far more likely to acquire a problem schema if two prior analogs were presented, and even more so if the abstract solution principle was presented as well.
- The importance of problem-solving schemas in physics has been shown by Chi, Feltovich and Glaser, who found that novice

physicists grouped problems according to surface features, while experts grouped them on the basis of fundamental laws of physics corresponding to the solution principles that should be used.

- Reed, Dempster and Ettinger point out that a single problem category may contain different types of problem. Once an analog is recognized, problem difficulty depends both on how similar the target problem is to the solution of a base problem and whether the solution is remembered.

5   A computer model of analogical problem solving

One problem with Gick and Holyoak's treatment of analogical problem solving is that assessments of analogous problems and solutions depend on intuition. For example, in their experiments, many of the subjects who proposed a convergence solution to the radiation problem indicated that the phrase in the fortress story about many roads radiating out from the fortress was critically important in suggesting the solution. Figure 2.2 suggests some of the processes involved in transforming the idea of roads radiating out from a fortress into a solution to the radiation problem (the arrows indicate transformation operators). Finding the solution involves inventing Ray Machines and transforming 'fortress' into 'tumour', and the roads into rays. Unfortunately, it remains a mystery how people are able to generate such transformations and inventions.

This issue of *how* analogy is used to construct a solution to a current problem has been explored by Carbonell (1983). In an

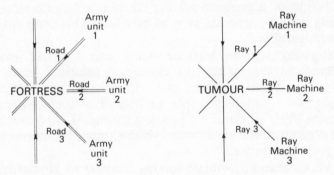

Figure 2.2

attempt to provide a rigorous specification of these solution processes, Carbonell has begun work on a computer model of analogical problem solving. Carbonell capitalizes on the idea that people are rarely confronted by truly novel problems, but rather that they meet variants of familiar problems throughout much of their lives. If you go shopping for a new washing machine you might find that the latest machines have features that weren't available on your old machine, but you will most likely be able to understand the new features by analogy. If you need to plan your first trip to Beirut, you could use your plan for a previous long-distance journey as a framework for solving the new problem.

The type of analogy problem that Carbonell tackles is much simpler than the problem dealt with by Gick and Holyoak. Carbonell's model deals with problems that have a great deal of surface similarity to previously solved problems, whereas Gick and Holyoak were concerned with analogous problems that had no common surface features. But, given our current state of knowledge about memory retrieval and analogical problem-solving processes, Carbonell's strategy is eminently sensible. The strategy involves working out the details of a process such as memory retrieval for a simple problem. The next step is to show that the details are correct by devising a computer program that is capable of memory retrieval. When the so-called easy problem has been solved, the goal would be to tackle a slightly harder problem. And the cycle would continue, tackling progressively harder problems.

In Carbonell's model, current problems are represented in working memory as structures containing an 'initial state' , a 'goal state', 'operators', 'operator restrictions' (these have been explained in Part I) and 'path constraints'. A path constraint is anything that limits the way a problem can be solved. An example of a path constraint would be a person's height when the goal is to paint a ceiling that is a few feet beyond his or her reach. An old, previously solved problem is represented by the same type of structures in long-term memory, where it is associated with its solution. Carbonell's program is designed to retrieve the solution to the old problem that most closely resembles the current problem. Retrieval of an appropriate old problem is achieved by the following matching operations:

1 matching the goal state of a current problem with goal states of old problems (I want to be rich);

2 matching the initial states of current and old problems (I'm broke and have some bills to pay);

3 matching old and new operator restrictions (my bills are due next week);

4 matching the path constraints required for a successful solution
with earlier examples (I can't use a public telephone for a long
distance call to a stranger unless I have a number of ten-pence
coins).

At this stage the four types of matching operations are given equal
weight. Figure 2.3 shows how a number of matches could be made
between a current travel problem and stored knowledge of 'old'
travel plans. In the example, the only link between the 'Current
problem' and 'Old plan (1)' is 'Initial state: Me at home'. There are
matches between the 'Current problem' and both 'Old plan (2)' and
'Old plan (3)': on both the 'Initial state: Me at home' and 'Operator
restrictions: Time limit: Arrive at "Goal" site in shortest possible
time'. However, there is an extra link between the 'Current problem'
and 'Old plan (2)': the link between 'Goal states', both of which
specify 'Intercity travel'. This example suggests that matches between goal states should be given considerable weight in a plan
retrieval process.

We will now look at how Carbonell's model uses the old problem
solution plan it has retrieved through matching. The basic principle
is that the solution of the problem is transformed to provide a solution to the current problem. Carbonell's model is in an early stage
of development and only a few of the processes described in the
following account have been incorporated in a running program.
This prototype program shows that the model is viable, but a considerable amount of work still needs to be done before the program
will be able to solve all of the kinds of problems discussed below. The
model is important because it specifies in some detail a number of
processes that might be involved in solution transformation in
analogical problem solving, and because it shows how the use of
analogy might be combined with the process of means-ends analysis
in solving problems. In the next section I will sketch out a few of the
solution transformation processes that Carbonell has identified and
begun to incorporate into his problem-solving program.

5.1   Solution transformation processes

In Carbonell's program, means-ends analysis serves a double
function. As well as being a method for solving problems in traditional problem spaces, such as those described in Part I, Carbonell
shows how means-ends analysis can operate in a problem space
where the initial state of the problem consists of a solution to an old
problem, and the goal state is a suitably transformed plan that meets

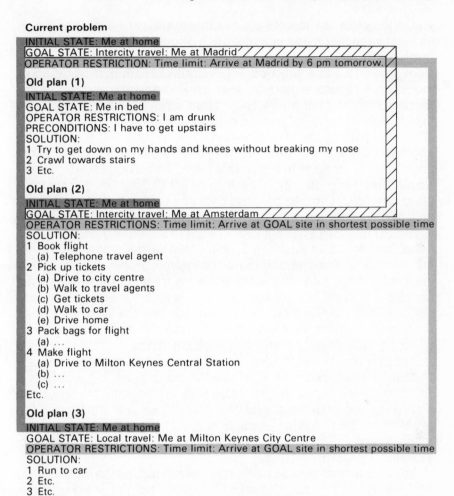

Current problem

INITIAL STATE: Me at home
GOAL STATE: Intercity travel: Me at Madrid
OPERATOR RESTRICTION: Time limit: Arrive at Madrid by 6 pm tomorrow.

Old plan (1)

INITIAL STATE: Me at home
GOAL STATE: Me in bed
OPERATOR RESTRICTIONS: I am drunk
PRECONDITIONS: I have to get upstairs
SOLUTION:
1 Try to get down on my hands and knees without breaking my nose
2 Crawl towards stairs
3 Etc.

Old plan (2)

INITIAL STATE: Me at home
GOAL STATE: Intercity travel: Me at Amsterdam
OPERATOR RESTRICTIONS: Time limit: Arrive at GOAL site in shortest possible time
SOLUTION:
1 Book flight
  (a) Telephone travel agent
2 Pick up tickets
  (a) Drive to city centre
  (b) Walk to travel agents
  (c) Get tickets
  (d) Walk to car
  (e) Drive home
3 Pack bags for flight
  (a) ...
4 Make flight
  (a) Drive to Milton Keynes Central Station
  (b) ...
  (c) ...
Etc.

Old plan (3)

INITIAL STATE: Me at home
GOAL STATE: Local travel: Me at Milton Keynes City Centre
OPERATOR RESTRICTIONS: Time limit: Arrive at GOAL site in shortest possible time
SOLUTION:
1 Run to car
2 Etc.
3 Etc.

Figure 2.3

the specifications of the current problem. Carbonell calls the problem space that transforms old problem solutions the *analogy transform problem space*. Operators in the analogy transform problem space insert, delete or modify one or more steps in the old plan. These operators are called *solution transformation operators*.

In short, Carbonell's program uses means-ends analysis to determine transformations that need to be made to an old plan to make it conform to current problem conditions. As a mundane example, imagine that you are about to finish work and have just heard a radio announcement that because of an accident there is a long tailback southbound on a certain section of the local motorway. Normally you drive onto the motorway, heading south, at, say, Junction 6, and leave the motorway at Junction 3. Junction 6 is just a few miles north of the tailback. As far as you know, the motorway is clear between Junction 5 and Junction 3. Given this situation, it might make more sense to alter a *part* of your usual plan for your homeward journey than to plan a new route from scratch. Since you want to avoid sitting in a traffic jam the best thing you could do would be to delete the part of the plan that takes you to Junction 6 and devise and insert a new plan part that takes you to Junction 5 instead. There are a number of ways in which this might be accomplished. For example, you might already know how to get to Junction 5 from your place of work. If so, the problem could be solved by (a) deleting the first part of your usual routine, which involves driving to Junction 6, and (b) inserting your plan for driving to Junction 5. If you didn't know how to get to Junction 5, you could devise a new plan using means-ends analysis in the more traditional problem space (get a local road map; find your work place on it; find Junction 5 on it; imagine a straight line between the two; search for main roads near the imagined straight line; and so on). Carbonell's program allows for such movement back and forth between the traditional problem space and the analogy transform problem space.

The best way to understand the solution transformation process is to look at a few examples. Carbonell's aim in analysing problems is to identify the kinds of processes that are logically necessary to transform old plans into something useful in new situations. The problem in the following example is useful because it suggests that a *parameter substitution operator* is an important factor in analogical problem solving.

Imagine a four-year-old boy who has a sudden desire for some cookies. Normally the child asks his mother but at the present time she is in another part of the house, out of sight, out of mind. The cookies are kept in a jar in a wall cupboard, far out of the child's reach. The child has not run into a similar problem in the past. The child could perhaps solve the problem using means-ends analysis in the traditional problem space, but Carbonell points out that problem solvers might also draw on vicariously acquired knowledge. For example, if the child had at some time in the past witnessed his father using a ladder to paint a ceiling, the child might be reminded of the incident. (How this reminding process works is an important issue which Carbonell has addressed, but which we will not discuss here.)

Imagine that the child remembers watching his father: (a) carrying a ladder into the house; (b) setting it up where the painting was to be done; (c) climbing the ladder; (d) and painting (as in Figure 2.4). Carbonell suggests that in order to use the plan suggested by his father's actions, the child would have to make a number of parameter substitutions such as substituting 'self' for 'father', and 'chair' for 'ladder'.

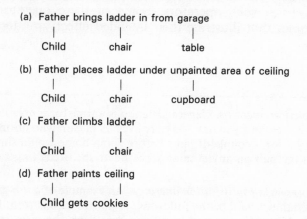

(a) Father brings ladder in from garage

 | | |
Child chair table

(b) Father places ladder under unpainted area of ceiling

 | | |
Child chair cupboard

(c) Father climbs ladder

 | |
Child chair

(d) Father paints ceiling

 | |
Figure 2.4   Child gets cookies

This *parameter substitution operator* is the kind of operator which we can all identify in our own activities, for example, when we use the blade of a knife as a screwdriver.

The effects of other transform space operators can be described with reference to the following example. Consider an old plan for doing your gardening, having the following five steps:

1 mow the lawn;
2 rake up grass from the lawn;
3 trim the hedges;
4 chat to the flowers;
5 turn on the sprinkler.

Now imagine that you trade in your old lawnmower for a model that collects grass as it cuts it. The old plan contains a step (step 2) which is no longer required, and requires a new step (for emptying the grass collector). Carbonell's model employs a number of 'insertion' and 'deletion' operators that are useful in modifying such old plans. The program employs a 'general deletion' operator that would simply get rid of any step that is no longer needed, such as step 2. An 'insertion' operator would add the new step of emptying the grass cutter. The new plan would look like this:

1 mow the lawn;
2 empty the grass cutter;
3 trim the hedges;
4 chat to the flowers;
5 turn on the sprinkler.

Through analysing a number of problems Carbonell has identified and described a number of transform space operators. Each transform space operator is specialized to transform particular differences between an old solution and the new problem. Carbonell describes eleven such operators. Some of these operators, along with examples that illustrate their intended effect, are described in Table 2.4.

Table 2.4

General deletion operator. General deletion is a transform operator that we all use fairly frequently in our everyday lives. A person who normally drops in to his local for a couple of pints before going home would simply delete his visit to the pub on any evening when he or she needs to get home in a hurry.

Sub-goal preserving substitution operator. An example of a sub-goal preserving substitution would be the following. A person travels from London to Edinburgh. Normally the person takes a taxi from the train station to a hotel. If the taxi drivers go on strike, the person does not want to give up the sub-goal of getting to a hotel, so the person could substitute 'take a bus' on the occasion of the taxi strike.

Initial segment concatenation operator. If you move house, and your new house has a garage whereas your previous house had only a carport, you would have to concatenate operations for unlocking and opening the garage door before parking, after which your standard parking plan could be put into operation. Such a change would also involve a *final segment concatenation* (adding something on to the end of an old plan): closing and locking the garage door.

Operator reordering operator. Imagine a person who has a set routine for morning activities: drop the kids off at school; drop the spouse off at work; stop at the garage if petrol is needed; drive to work. If petrol is very low one morning, the steps in the plan should be reordered so that the garage stop is made first. The reordering might also involve dropping the spouse off at work (if that is nearer to the petrol station) before dropping the children off at school.

Solution sequence truncation operator. This involves deleting unnecessary operators. My sons provide excellent examples all over the house. Putting the dishes away after they have been cleaned is apparently a stupid as well as unnecessary activity, because they would just have to be got out again the next time they are used.

Sequence inversion operator. Consider the problem of driving between two points in an unknown city. Once the problem is solved, the subsequent problem of returning to the departure site can be solved by operator sequence inversion (barring travel on one-way streets, and so forth).

SAQ 17

(a) Imagine that you have just disassembled a wardrobe in order to move it to another room. Which of the transform space operators in Table 2.4 could be used to devise a plan for reassembling the wardrobe after it has been moved?

(b) Consider a person who is in the habit of going to the cinema. Normally this person drives to the West End of London straight from work, parks his car, and queues for a ticket. Today he plans to see a particularly popular film and, because he is worried about getting a seat, telephones for a reservation before setting off. What kind of transform operator is reflected in this action?

(c) If the person in (b) cannot telephone for a reservation (because the cinema telephone is continuously engaged) but knows of someone who will be in the area of the cinema, he could ask that person to drop in and buy a ticket for him. Which transform space operator is the person using?

Summary of Section 5

- Carbonell devised a computer program to simulate analogical problem solving. Although the program has not been fully implemented, Carbonell provides details of a large number of processes for transforming old solutions to meet the specifications of new problems.

- The program incorporated procedures for accessing problem situations which are similar to the current problem by matching initial and goal states, operator restrictions and path constraints.

- Having identified the solution to a previous analogous problem, the program analyses differences between an old plan and problem specifications, and carries out appropriate transform space operations to modify, delete or insert elements to arrive at a new solution plan.

- In Carbonell's program, means-ends analysis operates in both traditional problem spaces and in a space of old problem solutions, called the analogy transform problem space.

6   Conclusions

We know a lot more today about analogical problem solving than we knew ten years ago. As described in Part I, we know that problem-solving strategies can be transferred between well-defined problem isomorphs if the conditions are right. The more recent research described in Part I attempts to detail the strategies used to solve these well-defined problems and how features of the task environment play a major role in determining the strategies.

Today we know that learning can also be transferred between ill-defined, distantly related problems, but that transfer is not automatic. People need experience with a number of examples of a particular type of problem in order to be able to abstract the common elements, to develop a problem schema, before they can automatically bring their knowledge to bear on subsequent problems. Processes involved in mapping analogs onto one another and in abstracting a generalized schema from a number of specific problem-solving instances, and the ways in which analogical problem solving and other problem-solving processes interact, are poorly understood. On the plus side, process models of analogical problem-solving processes have begun to appear. Over the next few years we can expect improvements in such models – improvements here meaning being better able to model human performance – once the prototypes have been built and their designers can afford to have more regard for human performance data. At the same time the computer models will suggest testable hypotheses about processes of interest. Improved models of memory organization and retrieval processes would have a major impact on such studies.

Part III
Representation and
Acquisition of
Cognitive Skills

Contents

Novice:

Roses are red
Violets are blue
All I think
About is you.

(HK)

Expert:

somewhere i have never travelled, gladly beyond
any experience, your eyes have their silence:
in your most frail gesture are things which enclose me,
or which i cannot touch because they are too near

your slightest look easily will unclose me
though i have closed myself as fingers,
you open always petal by petal myself as Spring opens
(touching skilfully, mysteriously) her first rose

or if your wish be to close me, i and
my life will shut very beautifully, suddenly,
as when the heart of this flower imagines
the snow carefully everywhere descending;

nothing which we are to perceive in this world equals
the power of your intense fragility: whose texture
compels me with the colour of its countries,
rendering death and forever with each breathing

(i do not know what it is about you that closes
and opens; only something in me understands
the voice of your eyes is deeper than all roses)
nobody, not even the rain, has such small hands

(e. e. cummings)

1   Introduction

Part III introduces recent research on learning, a relatively new focus of interest for cognitive psychologists. One of the attractions of puzzle problems like the Towers of Hanoi was the fact that they were novel problems which assumed no prior learning. Even the study of transfer effects was confined to the transfer of learning from one version of a problem to another. Yet in real life we gradually accumulate experience over many years as part of a learning process. We are all aware of the difference between a novice and an expert, whether driving a car, passing exams, or playing chess. Recall that in solving problems such as the Towers of Hanoi almost no knowledge beyond that provided by the experimenter is needed; although perhaps you did feel yourself to be more of an 'expert' in tackling such problems by the time you finished Part I. But, of course, in ordinary, mundane situations people bring a lot of previously acquired knowledge to bear both in understanding the problem and in solving it. So the puzzle problems are not very representative of real-life problem solving.

Bhaskar and Simon (1977) discussed the extension of problem-solving research to *semantically rich domains*, domains of knowledge in which substantial amounts of prior information are necessary to tackle problems. An example of such a domain is geometry. Problem solving in geometry requires a great deal of domain specific knowledge which has to be learnt, and in that respect it is a semantically rich domain. But it is also what Larkin (1981) has called a *formal domain*. Formal domains are domains that (a) involve a great deal of knowledge and (b) depend on generally agreed logical principles sufficient to solve problems in that domain.

An example of a domain that is semantically rich but is not a formal domain, according to Larkin's definition, is psychology. In order to see this, all you have to do is listen to a behaviourist and a psychoanalyst arguing about the best way to treat neurotic symptoms. Both have a great deal of knowledge but there are no agreed principles for solving the problem.

Beginning in the late seventies and continuing up to the present day numerous studies have been conducted into the differences between the problem-solving strategies and knowledge structures of novices and experts in domains as varied as physics, architecture and computer programming. Investigators were able to see clear differences in solving problems between novices, intermediate learners and experts; the next step was to ask how expertise was acquired from prior learning experiences. This was the step that led cognitive psychologists to show an interest in *learning processes*. In contrast to the earlier emphasis on modelling *performance processes*, as for example in Polson's model of problem solving which we discussed in Part I, psychologists are now concerned with *changes* in performance that occur as an individual is transformed progressively from a novice to an expert.

2 Novices and experts

Research has been carried out in several different domains of knowledge, in all of which it is assumed that there are large differences in knowledge between experts, intermediate learners and novices. In this section we shall discuss the domains of chess and computer programming, physics and architecture.

2.1 Chess

In 1973 Chase and Simon reported an interesting series of experiments (Chase and Simon, 1973a; 1973b) in which they investigated the ability of chess players of different abilities to reconstruct positions on a game board after being given a very brief period of time for viewing the board. One of their experiments, the 'memory' experiment, was a replication of an experiment first performed by de Groot (1965). This experiment is described in Techniques Box D.

TECHNIQUES BOX D

Chase and Simon's memory experiment

Rationale
The basic idea was to see whether acquiring expert knowledge of a domain changes the way the information from that domain is organized in memory.

Method
Chase and Simon presented three subjects – a beginner, a class A player, and a Master – with five 'middle-game' positions (with about twenty-five pieces still remaining on the board) and five 'end-game' positions (with about fourteen pieces still remaining on the board). These were taken from positions in actual games discussed in books on chess. They also presented four 'meaningless' middle-game and end-game positions by randomly rearranging the same number of chess pieces on the board.

Subjects were provided with an empty chessboard and a full set of chess pieces. For each trial they were allowed five seconds to view one of the prepared positions, and then, after the position board had been removed, they were asked to reconstruct the position they had seen on their empty board. If a subject failed to reconstruct the position accurately, their board was cleared, the game position was re-presented, and the subject again attempted to reconstruct the entire position from memory. This procedure was repeated until the position was perfectly recalled.

Results
Figure 3.1 presents the results for recall of the middle games and end games.

Figure 3.1 shows that on average both the class A player and the beginner required seven trials to reconstruct middle-game positions,

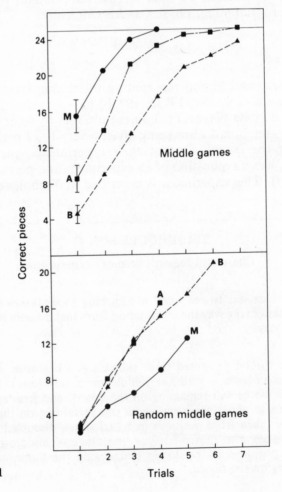

Figure 3.1

while the Master required only four trials. On end-game positions (not shown in Figure 3.1) the Master was able to reconstruct positions with an average of three trials, while the class A player and the beginner required four and six trials, respectively.

The most dramatic difference between the subjects, however, was in the number of pieces correctly placed on the first trial. Figure 3.1 shows that in the middle-game positions, the Master was able to place about sixteen pieces, while the class A player correctly recalled, on average, eight pieces, and the beginner only four pieces. In the end-game reconstructions the Master recalled, on average, eight pieces, the class A player seven pieces, and the beginner four pieces. Interestingly, the superiority of the Master over the other subjects was not maintained beyond the first trial. On subsequent trials, when the subjects were able to see the position boards again, the Master usually added about four more pieces whereas the other subjects were able to add about five or six pieces on the second and subsequent trials.

The results from the reconstructions of meaningless, or random, positions show that players of all levels of skill were lucky to recall three pieces accurately on the first trial, and things did not greatly improve in this condition on any of the subsequent trials.

One possible explanation for the Master's ability to recall twice as much as the class A player and four times as much as the beginner on the first trial for meaningful positions is that the Master has a very large (visual) short-term memory span. Perhaps skill in chess is correlated with superior short-term memory capacity. Chase and Simon were able to discount this explanation of the Master's performance because of the results from the reconstructions of meaningless, or random, positions. In this situation the results show that experts were no better at reconstructing positions than novices.

On the basis of these results, Chase and Simon hypothesized that in real-game situations, highly skilled players perceive *relations* between pieces, whereas duffers perceive little more than the positions of individual pieces on the board. De Groot had suggested that a Master's long-term memory contains a vast array of stored patterns. These patterns are memory representations of legitimate meaningful board positions that are categorized in terms of clusters of pieces attacking or defending each other. Perceived board positions could be recognized as matching stored memory representations.

Chase and Simon estimated that a chess Master has stored in memory 50,000 to 100,000 such patterns, or 'chunks' of information as they called them. If you think this sounds like a ridiculous claim, remember that the vocabulary of a university educated person is estimated to be about 50,000 to 100,000 words. Thus, just as an experienced reader is presumed to have word recognition units for thousands of letter patterns, or chunks (that is, words), the chess Master is presumed to have pattern recognition units for 'pawn chain', 'castled-king position' and many other chess positions. The difference between the pattern recognition abilities of the skilled and unskilled chess player would be like the difference between the word recognition abilities of university educated adults and the recognition of individual letters by primary school children. Besides knowing more individual words, the adult is likely to recognize whole chunks of commonly occurring words.

In order to discover exactly what these chunks of information might be, Chase and Simon devised a perception task. In this experiment subjects were videotaped while they reconstructed positions on a board – as in the memory experiment – but this time the subjects were allowed to glance back at the original board position as often as they wished. The presumption was that, each time the subject glanced at the board, he would encode one meaningful pattern (reflecting one chunk stored in long-term memory). Chase and Simon analysed groups of pieces placed on the reconstruction board after each glance and found that the most frequently occurring patterns for the Master were (a) pawn chains, (b) castled-king positions, (c) clusters of pieces of the same colour, (d) attack, and (e) defence relations. The less skilled players also appeared to use some of the same chunks, but each chunk contained fewer pieces than the chunks of the Master.

In further experiments Chase and Simon also demonstrated that, as well as knowing about relational patterns between chess pieces, chess Masters know stereotyped sequences of moves. In one experiment, a novice, an expert and a Master were required to memorize a twenty-five move game (actually fifty moves, as the moves of both players were counted as one move in the experiment). The Master required only ten minutes to learn the moves, while the class A player and the novice took half an hour and an hour and a half respectively. The Master made only four errors in learning the move sequence, the class A player made thirteen errors, and the novice made ninety-four errors.

In summary, Chase and Simon argued that the superior performance of a chess Master, by comparison with less able players, is a result of the Master's perception of patterns consisting of complex attack, defence and other relations between pieces on a chessboard during a game. These perceived patterns depend on the way a chess Master's knowledge is organized in long-term memory. Non-expert players, on the other hand, either have not yet acquired knowledge of meaningful configurations of pieces, or have not yet learned how to utilize this knowledge.

This research draws our attention to the importance of knowledge in skilled problem solving. Research on puzzle-like problems stressed processes such as means-ends analysis. Research on chess suggests that processes like this may be only the first resort of unknowledgeable players. When we know nothing about a problem, such as the Waterjugs problem, we have to work out from first principles a sequence of 'best' moves. But when we are faced with a problem we have experienced often before we can 'run off' patterns of already learnt responses. Since most of the 'problems' we encounter in real life are analogous to previous experience, we are already prepared with the necessary knowledge; although, as was demonstrated in Part II, people do not always appreciate analogies or know how to apply solutions. However, in a situation like chess, which has stereotyped sequences of moves, an expert can classify game situations in terms of known patterns of play, and is able to call on stored knowledge of how to deal with new situations that arise.

2.2   Computer programming

In the domain of computer programming, McKeithen, Reitman, Rueter and Hirtle (1981) asked groups of computer programmers of different levels of skill to recall computer programs that were presented briefly on a computer's visual display unit. Just as Chase and Simon presented both meaningful and non-meaningful chess positions, McKeithen *et al.* presented meaningful computer programs and programs in which lines of instructions had been randomly scrambled. They found that expert programmers were extraordinarily good at recalling meaningful programs. Novice programmers performed very poorly on this task, and intermediate-level programmers performed about half-way between the novices and experts. However, experts were no better than anyone else at recalling the scrambled programs.

McKeithen *et al.* argued that the performance of the experts was based on the organization of their knowledge in long-term memory. They tested the hypothesis by asking the different groups of subjects to memorize and recall lists of programming 'keywords' — elementary computer program instructions and concepts, such as 'string', 'real' 'bits', 'false', 'while', 'and', 'or' and 'do' — and analysed the order in which the keywords were recalled by the different groups.

They found that experts organized the material for recall in a way that reflected meaningful programming relationships between the words (for example, 'while', 'do', 'for' and 'step') while novices organized the words according to natural language associations. For example, many novices would recall 'bits', 'of' and 'string' together, three words which when put together like that have an obvious meaning to most people but which make up a meaningless combination in terms of computer programming. McKeithen *et al.* argued that such recall orders reflected the unorganized nature of the novices' knowledge of programming.

In another experiment on novice and expert computer programmers, Adelson (1981) used a free recall task in order to uncover the underlying organization of knowledge of her subjects. Adelson presented her subjects with sixteen lines of code from the PPL programming language. The sixteen lines of code were taken from three real programs, but she presented the lines of code in scrambled order. All subjects were allowed to view the sixteen lines of code for twenty seconds, and were then given eight minutes to recall all they could. Each subject went through eight such trials, each time with twenty seconds viewing time and eight minutes recall time. Adelson showed that, as trials proceeded, experts started to group together the lines of code that 'belonged together' in the original three routines. In contrast, novice programmers grouped together lines of code that looked alike.

Adelson argued that experts used their knowledge of the various routines to organize the lines of program code into sensible groupings that belonged to particular routines. This research provides additional support for the hypothesis that experts have a hierarchy of knowledge about a domain which enables them to organize clusters of information into higher order structures, like chess games and computer programs. It is these functional information structures that give experts such a great advantage over novices in a wide range of tasks. In the terminology of schema theory it could be said that the experts have more highly organized *schemas*, which represent their knowledge structures about a particular domain. There is a fuller discussion of the role of schemas in representing knowledge structures in another volume in the Open Guides to Psychology series – Cohen, Eysenck and Le Voi (1985).

In research into differences between novices and experts in other domains, such as physics and architecture, the same pattern of results has emerged. One major difference between novices and experts is that experts can rely on memorized solutions to many problems in their domain (this is one of the reasons they are experts), while novices can seldom call on a very large store of answers to the problems with which they are confronted. However, there are differences in the strategies used by novices and experts to solve problems even when the expert can't simply retrieve the solution from memory. Bhaskar and Simon (1977) have shown that experts work 'forwards' to find a problem solution, using the material presented in a problem statement to make inferences about information that will be needed to solve a problem. Novices, on the other hand, tend to work 'backwards' from the goal or use means-ends analysis for trying out and evaluating different operations. However, when experts are put into domain related task situations with which they are unfamiliar, they too tend to fall back on means-ends analysis as a general problem-solving method.

A lot of recent research has shown that there are important differences between the way novices and experts *represent* a problem. Simon and Simon (1978) found evidence for such differences in their research on problem solving by a novice and an expert in physics. Their novice subject went straight to work on the problem after reading the problem statement, but the expert first worked on constructing a more concrete representation of the problem. More recently Chi, Feltovich and Glaser (1981), in a mammoth study of the differences between novices and experts in solving physics problems, have shown that novices try to understand a problem by paying attention to the kinds of objects mentioned in the problem statement rather than relating the objects to deep, underlying principles as experts do.

While all of the results presented above are interesting because they point to knowledge organization and knowledge specific problem-solving processes, we should keep in mind that the mechanisms are inferred from differences in the performance of experts and novices on various tasks. For example, we have spoken confidently of 'expert organizations of knowledge', 'chunks of knowledge about relational patterns between pieces on a chessboard', and so on. But what really do we mean by these statements? Is there any way of being more specific? It is easy to hypothesize that a chess Master has the ability to recognize an 'attack' relation between pieces on a chess board, but much harder to show how this ability is actually represented and used. Which specific conditions do people respond to, whether expert or novice, in particular task situations? What we need is a method for representing skills directly, a problem to which we will now turn.

Summary of Section 2

- Research in a number of different domains such as chess and computer programming indicates that skilled performance is based on highly organized domain specific knowledge. Experts have a store of patterns representing commonly occurring configurations of information in the knowledge domain, and a store of solutions/operations to apply to them.
- One difference between novices and experts is the way they represent problems. Experts classify problems within their domain in terms of underlying principles and spend time reformulating problems during problem solving.
- Another difference is in terms of the strategies employed. Experts tend to work 'forwards' while novices tend to work 'backwards' from the goal, or use means-ends analysis in solving problems.

3 Computer models of problem solving

In Part I we discussed the computer programs devised by Newell and Simon to model problem solving on the Towers of Hanoi problem, and by Polson and his associates to model the behaviour of people solving Waterjug problems. It is time to consider the notion of computer models a little more closely.

Most computer programs consist of a linear sequence of instructions, containing branching points. The branching points allow some flexibility in a program, directing the program to perform one set of instructions if a particular condition holds at the branching point (for example, if the contents of a specified register contain a number greater than 100, call sub-routine 'X'), or to follow another set of instructions if a different condition holds. Such programs are usually hierarchically organized, with a main *procedure* which calls *sub-procedures*, which in their own turn may call other *sub-procedures*, and so on. These are also called *routines* and *sub-routines*. You can think of cooking a meal as an example of running such a program. Making spaghetti involves a number of sub-procedures such as collecting together the ingredients, making a sauce, and cooking the spaghetti. The main procedure guides the organization of the various sub-procedures. When a procedure calls a sub-procedure, the sub-procedure takes control of processing until it completes the process it was designed to perform and then passes control back to the calling procedure. This calling of sub-procedures by each other can continue to any depth according to the number and ordering of branching points in the program. Such programs can be described as remorseless. That is, if you run such a program, it will run from beginning to end regardless of whatever else is going on in the world around it. Other programs that you want to run have to wait their turn. Such programs have very great powers of directing attention to a single current goal.

Contrast this notion with your own intuitions about the nature of human attentional processes. People are continually bombarded by external events, some of which they pay attention to and some of which they ignore. People have the ability to shift attention from a current goal when more important events occur in their surroundings. If you are in the middle of solving the Towers of Hanoi problem, your ability to survive would be seriously impaired if you had to see the problem through to the end before you could respond to somebody shouting 'Fire!'.

It is for this reason that hierarchically organized, unstoppable programs are poor tools for devising models of general human cognition. Another reason is that it is exceedingly difficult to see how learning might be modelled by such programs. Since these programs are organized as a single overall hierarchy of program instructions, altering them to account for a newly learned problem-solving strategy involves changes throughout the program. Yet, one of the central facts of learning is that it occurs piecemeal. Learning often seems to involve small increments to a knowledge base, or continual small improvements in ability to apply knowledge which has already been acquired. What is needed to model human learning is a type of computer programming which contains lots of separate rules for dealing with situations any one of which can be altered independently to adapt to new situations.

3.1   Production systems

In recent years, cognitive psychologists have begun to model performance and learning processes using programming of this kind, which is known as *production systems*.

Production systems were first introduced to psychologists as frameworks for implementing cognitive theories by Newell and Simon in their book *Human Problem Solving* (1972). Production system models of cognition are based on the idea that knowledge is represented in long-term memory in the form of *condition/action rules*. Each of these rules, called *productions*, specifies the exact conditions in which an action should take place. A set of related productions constitutes a production system. The production system approach has wide application and can give an account of much everyday behaviour as well as formal problem-solving tasks. For instance, if you hear someone shouting 'Fire', this is the *condition* for the *action* of raising the alarm yourself. The general notion is that behaviour is a response to a current situation. In Section 2 it was stressed that a chess expert responds to complex patterns on a game board; in other words a certain configuration of pieces provides the condition that triggers a particular action in the expert's repertoire. Although few of us are chess experts or expert computer programmers, we are all experts in a thousand different things we do. Even infants have some expertise. The following production system might represent knowledge which a newborn infant has about how to deal with discomfort or pain.

Production 1
Condition: IF you are in a state having a negative feeling

Action: THEN wriggle about

Production 2
Condition: IF you are in a state having a negative feeling
            and you are wriggling about

Action: THEN cry

Production 3
Condition: IF you are in a state having a negative feeling
            and you are wriggling about
            and you are crying

Action: THEN scream and kick the crib to pieces

These productions provide a graduated set of responses to many situations over which the infant has no direct control, and which accomplish the goal of having someone intervene on her behalf. The condition 'IF you are in a state having a negative feeling' would correspond to a number of situations in which the infant might find herself (for example, the irritation of wet nappies, hunger or boredom). Any of these would trigger the first production. If the infant continues to feel negative (that is, no one comes) even when she is wriggling, this will be the condition for triggering Production 2, and so on.

Productions systems are a lot like the *S-R rules* of learning theory (see another volume in The Open Guides to Psychology series, Greene and Hicks, 1984, for a review). The 'IF' part of a rule is like the 'stimulus' part of an S-R pair; the 'THEN' part is like the response. However, there are important differences between production systems and *stimulus-response theories*. One crucial difference is that stimulus-response theories are concerned with observable, external stimuli and observable responses. Production systems are concerned with observable behaviour, for example crying, but also with mental events that occur within the organism, for example, negative feelings or retrieving knowledge from long-term memory.

3.2   Production system architecture

So far we have been talking about production rules in the abstract. But what mechanisms would be needed to implement such a system? Whether one is considering a computer or a human being, there is a certain organizational structure required to produce actions in response to conditions. This is known as the *production system architecture*. Such an architecture must include a *production memory,* in which the condition/action rules are stored, a *working memory*, in which current conditions can be temporarily held, and, finally, *activation rules* for retrieving the appropriate stored production in order to select an appropriate action for the current conditions. For instance, stored in production memory would be the production:

> IF you see a fire
>
> THEN holler 'Fire'

Thus, when a 'fire' situation is perceived it is held in working memory as a current condition. The activation rules then search through production memory to find a production that links an action to a fire condition. Finding the current condition matches the condition of the fire production, the corresponding action 'holler "fire"' is initiated.

1   Production memory
The *production memory* simply contains lists of productions incorporating condition/action (IF/THEN) rules. The rules represent the system's procedural knowledge, knowledge about how to get things done, and what to do when the system is confronted by particular situations. One particular rule might be:

> IF you are going out
>   and it is raining
>
> THEN wear a raincoat
>   and take an umbrella

113

Production memory may or may not be organized (according to the preferences or theoretical position of the system builder). That is, rules might be grouped together in terms of goals they help to satisfy, (for example, 'self preservation') or in terms of key words (for example, 'rain'), or may simply be added to the system one after the other as they are acquired.

2   Working memory

In production systems, *working memory* is a database of symbols on which the system can operate at any given point in time. As an illustration, let's assume that you are getting ready to go to work, and that you know it is raining outside. Working memory includes all the information about conditions which is currently active. (The brackets containing dots indicate other information currently active in working memory, for example, the kids are screaming at one another, you want to remember to buy some cigarettes on the way to work, and so on.)

>   (I am going out)
>   (It is raining)
>   (... ... ...)
>   (... ... ...)
>   (... ... ...)
>   (... ... ...)

3   Activation rules

Assuming that we have information about current conditions in working memory and appropriate IF/THEN rules in production memory, the next question to consider is the all important one of how we activate an appropriate rule for dealing with the situation. If a problem solver sees chess pieces on a board (that is, current conditions in working memory), how does he or she know which action should be activated to make the next move? In order to get any behaviour from a production system we need to have *activation rules* for comparing the contents of working memory with the condition element of the productions in production memory. The activation rule states that when any pattern in working memory matches the IF conditions of a production, the production 'fires' the THEN action. As soon as the action is performed, the *pattern matching* cycle is begun again. If the contents of working memory include 'it is raining' and 'I am going out', the activation rules will find that these match the conditions of a production and so will activate the actions 'wear a raincoat' and 'take an umbrella'.

4   Conflict resolution rules

Production systems need some way of deciding what to do when two or more rules are applicable to a particular situation. Suppose the conditions in working memory include the fact that you are about to miss your bus to work and the telephone rings as you are going through the door. One of these events meets the conditions of the production in production memory: *IF the phone rings THEN you should answer it*; the other event meets the condition for *IF you are in a hurry to get somewhere THEN you should rush*. Which rule should you apply in such a situation? This depends on the conflict resolution rules you have for resolving such conflicts. If you have a rule that gives priority to punctuality at work, that rule can be used to resolve the conflict over whether you should continue to go through the door or stop to answer the telephone.

There are a number of ways of resolving conflicts between rules, including recency, specificity and refractoriness, as in the following examples.

The *recency rule* is a conflict resolution rule which states that if more than one rule applies to the contents of working memory, then choose the rule that applies to the most recently entered items in working memory. The justification for this rule is that the behaviour generated will reflect the most recent and, therefore, probably the most urgent event, for example, a fire.

The *specificity rule* is based on the notion that more specific rules reflect more of the characteristics of a particular situation and hence are more likely to be appropriate to that situation. Consider the following situation: you want to get the milk from the doorstep and you know it is raining outside. The rule about what to do when going outside in the rain applies, but most of us wouldn't want to put on a raincoat and unfurl an umbrella in this situation. Presumably we have more specific rules to cover such situations, such as:

> IF   you are going out
> and it is raining
> and you will only be outside for a few moments
> THEN   duck in and out as quickly as possible

Specific rules give more details about the exact contexts in which particular actions are appropriate.

The *refractoriness rule* is an important conflict resolution rule. It states that if the conflict would activate a rule (or rules) that applied on the immediately preceding cycle, then it should not be applied again. This kind of rule prevents a system from getting itself entwined in a loop, repeatedly applying the same rule to the contents of working memory. In such a case another of the possible rules in the production memory would be selected for activation. This rule for avoiding recent actions does not necessarily conflict with the recency rule since this is applied to recent conditions. What it would do is to prevent you constantly unfurling more and more umbrellas because it is still raining.

When a rule has been chosen, the action on the 'THEN' part of the rule is executed. Actions, like conditions, can be arbitrarily complex. The actions can be motor responses (for example, summarize something just read, write an answer) or mental responses (for example, add a new item of information to long-term memory or to working memory). Once the action has been performed, the whole cycle starts again. New additions to the contents of working memory will change the current conditions on which the system operates and so become the basis for the activation of another production on the next cycle.

SAQ 18
In order to test your understanding of production systems, create a production set that reflects a skill possessed by most people in the United Kingdom: making a cup of tea. Imagine that you are making a cup of tea (using a teabag) for somebody who likes milk and two sugars. You should begin by listing the components of the skill: switching on the kettle, putting the teabag into the cup (at the right time), and so on. Then for each component write out a set of condition/action rules.
Here's a couple of rules to get you started:

> IF   your goal is to boil a kettle of water
>   and the kettle is empty
>
> THEN   set as a goal to fill the kettle with water
>
> IF   your goal is to boil a kettle of water
>   and the kettle is full
>
> THEN   set as a goal to plug the kettle into a source of electricity
>   and make sure the electricity switch is on

3.3   Production systems and learning

Modelling human learning is one of the harder problems in psychology and one on which cognitive psychologists have only recently begun to focus their attention. The production systems I have described so far have not attempted to model learning, but rather assume that all productions are already stored in production memory waiting to be activated. If a production system is to model learning, then new productions must somehow be added to the system's production memory. This idea, that human learning may consist of the piecemeal addition of new productions for performing actions in response to certain conditions, has thrown new light on learning processes.

To show how production systems can model learning by the addition of new productions, I will describe a study performed by Anzai and Simon (1979) in which they observed a single subject learning to solve the five-rings Towers of Hanoi (TOH) problem. The subject made four attempts at the problem. On each attempt the subject used a different strategy. Anzai and Simon constructed production systems to simulate each of the subject's four different strategies, and then set themselves the task of modelling the learning involved in transforming each strategy into its successor.

The subject's initial strategy, reflected in the first production system model constructed by Anzai and Simon, involved an exploration of the problem space, with little or no planning of moves. Anzai and Simon called this initial exploration of the problem space a *selective search strategy*. Although the subject (and the production system model) did not know what constituted a 'good' move on the first attempt at the problem, she did have a few quite general *domain independent* problem-solving strategies which allowed her to detect 'bad' moves. These general strategies included the idea that you should avoid returning to an earlier state of a problem (a loop avoidance strategy) and the notion that you shouldn't make a sequence of moves which leads to a state that could be reached by a shorter sequence. These general strategies helped the subject to acquire domain specific rules which could be used to narrow the search space on subsequent attempts at the problem.

We can understand better the effect of general strategies in learning if we look at the sequence of moves the subject made on her first attempt. The subject made eleven moves in all, as indicated in Figure 3.2 In the figure, the pegs are called A, B and C. The five rings are numbered 1 to 5, from smallest to largest. At the start of the problem the rings were all stacked up on peg A, and the goal was to move them to peg C.

		Ring	From peg	To peg
1	move	1	A	B
2	move	2	A	C
3	move	1	B	C
4	move	3	A	B
5	move	1	C	A
6	move	2	C	B
7	move	1	A	B
8	move	4	A	C
9	move	1	B	A
10	move	2	B	C
11	move	2	C	B

Figure 3.2

The first step in the TOH problem is one of the few real choice points in the problem. When a TOH problem involves an odd number of rings, the appropriate first move is to move the smallest ring to the goal peg (peg C, in this case). The subject did not know this, and chose to move the smallest ring to the middle peg (peg B) as she said in her verbal protocol, in order to 'keep the goal peg free for the larger rings'.

In moves 2 to 10 there is some evidence of look-ahead in choosing moves. For example, at move 3 the subject had the choice of moving the smallest ring (1) either back to peg A or on to peg C. If she had chosen to move it to peg A, she would have blocked the movement of ring 3. But she chose to move the smallest ring to peg C, so that she could next move ring 3 to peg B. Following this move, the subject performed a sequence of moves that allowed her to move ring 4 to the goal peg (at move 8). But at this point in the problem the subject realized that she had blocked the possibility of moving the largest ring (5) to the goal peg. She then had the idea of moving the pyramid of rings on peg B (rings 1, 2 and 3) out of the way so she could move ring 4 off the goal peg. But she did not really know how to achieve this goal. The final two moves consituted a loop, in which she moved ring 2 from peg B to peg C and back again. At this point the subject decided to give up her first attempt and start again.

Anzai and Simon suggested that people have general schemas for detecting loops in problem solving and proposed that when they are detected, a domain specific rule is created to avoid such loops on future attempts at the problem. The general production for loop-avoidance might look something like this:

> IF   you are considering performing action X
>   and the previous action, action Y, is the inverse of
>   action X
> THEN   exclude action X
>   and generate an alternative action

In order to avoid looping moves in the future, a new production rule should be constructed that allows moves to be generated and evaluated before they are actually made. In fact, the learning system designed by Anzai and Simon does just this. The system embeds details of 'bad' move sequences into the general rule, and adds this new rule to the domain specific stock of rules for solving the TOH problem. The new rule might look something like the following:

> IF   you are considering performing move 2 C B
>   and the previous move was move 2 B C

THEN   exclude move 2 C B
       and generate an alternative move

The learning system devised by Anzai and Simon also contains rules
for detecting sequences of moves that are longer than they need be,
such as when the same ring is moved twice in succession. Rules are
created for avoiding such moves in future by a process like that used
in the creation of the loop avoidance rule.

The effect of such domain specific rules is to guide search and lead
the problem solver ever forward in the problem. For example, the
loop avoidance rule and the rule that prevents over-long move
sequences would lead a solver from state 2 in the problem (see Figure
3.3) to state 4, because the other two possible moves represent either
a loop (a return to state 1) or an over-long move sequence (to state 3).

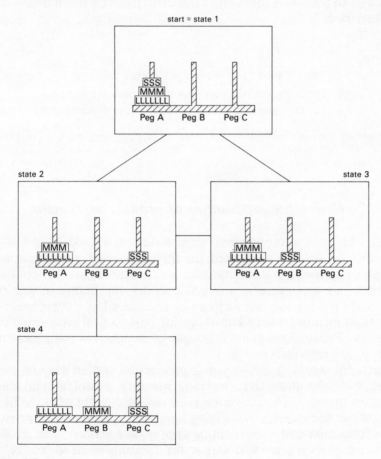

Figure 3.3

If a solver manages to use strategies to eliminate backward and sideways moves, and thus only moves forward, there is a high likelihood that he or she will acquire some understanding of the shortest solution path and hence develop a more sophisticated strategy for the next attempt at the problem. For instance, Anzai and Simon's subject found that moving ring 4 to the goal peg (C) blocked her ability to move the largest ring. To avoid this, ring 4 should be moved to the spare peg (B). On the next attempt at the problem, the subject could then set up a sub-goal of moving ring 4 to the spare peg, and thus try to plan a sequence of moves for achieving this specific sub-goal.

This example illustrated the notion of learning through adaptation of production systems by adding new productions to the system. This is only one way in which production systems have been used to model learning. In Section 4 some more powerful learning mechanisms will be described.

SAQ 19
(a) If you were solving the 8, 5, 3 Waterjugs problem, and your first move was:
> pour five litres from the eight-litre jug into the five-litre jug,

how would the loop avoidance strategy help you decide which move to make next?

(b) What are the other possible moves, once the looping move has been excluded?

3.4   Psychological implications of production systems

While the production system architecture described above is in principle an abstract one, used for the purpose of implementing a computer program, it is natural for psychologists to consider whether this architecture is a good model for human cognition. Obviously production memory can be considered as a component of long-term memory where knowledge of how to deal with situations is stored. Productions can be thought of as schemas for generating appropriate responses.

Next, the working memory in a production system may be compared with the short-term working memory postulated in many cognitive theories. The activation rules can be thought of as the basic processing mechanisms underlying cognition, processes for retrieving information and implementing appropriate actions. The conflict resolution rules represent strategies for choosing what to 'notice' or 'think about' next, and thus function like attention mechanisms.

Note that the production systems approach has not concerned itself with issues about the capacity limitations of working memory. In the production system architecture described so far, working memory can be virtually limitless, yet all the evidence from psychological investigations suggests a limited capacity of human short-term memory. (Recall the discussion of Polson's model of performance on transformation problems presented in Part I, Section 5.1.) These issues must, of course, arise if production systems are regarded as a model of human cognition. So, to simulate human problem solving, the model would have to incorporate a limit to the number of conditions which could be contained in working memory at any one time.

Another important feature of production system architecture is that each production is completely independent of the others, and can thus be seen as a single component of the total problem-solving process. This characteristic, known as *modularity*, is not nearly as evident in other programming languages. It has the virtue that brand new production rules can be added into production rule memory in order to bring about improved performance of the model without having to alter previously existing production rules. The associated difficulty, of course, is that the more rules there are, the greater the chance of rule conflict occurring as a result of many rules being activated by the same conditions. For instance, further along in the TOH problem, a solver might infer another strategy for selecting a first move which would conflict with an earlier strategy. The need to build in conflict resolution rules can make a production system unwieldy and leads to the temptation to add lots of *ad hoc* rules to get the program to work.

Production systems, because of the particular architecture underlying them, lend themselves nicely to cognitive models in which the role of short-term or working memory can be made explicit, and to models of learning which might be expressed in terms of new production rules being added to long-term memory.

Summary of Section 3

- Production systems provide a powerful tool for modelling learned behaviour which occurs in response to current situations, such as expert performance in the game of chess.
- Production system architecture consists of production rules in production memory and current conditions in working memory. Activation rules match the current conditions to productions

which activate appropriate actions. Conflict resolution rules help the system select a single appropriate action when more than one production rule matches the current conditions.

- Production system architecture encourages parallels with human cognitive processing: production memory with long-term memory, working memory with short-term memory, activation rules with processes of pattern recognition.
- Production systems are especially suited to models in which the role of short-term or working memory needs to be made explicit, or models in which the process of 'learning' can be thought of in terms of adding new productions to long-term memory.
- There are also certain disadvantages involved in using production systems. The addition of many new production rules may lead to tricky rule conflict situations.

4   ACT: a cognitive theory of learning

Section 2 presented evidence from domains such as chess, physics and computer programming which indicates that expert problem solving depends on already stored domain specific knowledge. However, in Section 3 the case was made that such knowledge might be in the form of production rules for dealing with particular situations. Ironically, prior knowledge stored in long-term memory, which is normally thought to influence behaviour in a top-down direction, may be in the form of productions which operate in a much more bottom-up direction, that is, the selection of productions is driven by the current situation. In other words, an expert's knowledge consists of rules for recognizing and dealing with a large number of patterns. Indeed, in many situations an expert does not have to 'solve' a problem at all, since he or she already knows how to respond to many situations in his or her area of expertise. A novice, on the other hand, spends a lot of time searching for a solution to a problem. So, what have experts learnt which enables them to generate appropriate responses in a large number of situations?

In this section I want to introduce you to a theory of learning called ACT which has been developed by John Anderson. The theory attempts to account for the full range of cognitive functioning, from pattern recognition through to problem solving, and has in fact undergone a number of reformulations over the years. Because of the wide range of ACT's application, it is not possible to describe the theory here in any great detail. (There is a very readable, and highly recommended, account of the most recent version of Anderson's theory, called ACT*, or ACT star, in his book *The Architecture of Cognition*, 1983).

Anderson subscribes to the view of expertise presented in Section 2 above, and has set as one of his goals to demonstrate that his theory of learning, as embodied in ACT, can explain how a large domain-specific database and specialized problem-solving procedures could be acquired by a system that starts off with only a few facts about the domain of learning, and general problem-solving procedures such as those described in our discussion of problem solving in toy worlds – working backwards, working forwards, analogy and means-ends analysis.

4.1 Declarative and procedural knowledge

As an example of an expert performance, consider the duties of the cabin staff on an aeroplane. Cabin staff have to deal with situations as varied as distributing meals within a set amount of time, caring for sick passengers (anything from drunkenness to contagious diseases), decompression, emergency landings, and fires.

Each of these tasks is composed of a number of activities that have to be coordinated and swiftly executed. For instance, if a member of the cabin staff notices smoke coming from an oven in the galley he or she should switch off the oven, pull the circuit breaker, isolate the area (remove anything that is combustible, including people), get the fire extinguisher, and get someone (not a passenger) to inform the flight deck. He or she *should not* open the oven door, and should use the fire extinguisher only if flames appear. Efficient performance depends on knowing how to switch off the oven; knowing where the nearest fire extinguisher is, how to unfasten it from its fitting, and how to use it if necessary; and knowing how to inform other members of the staff without terrifying the passengers.

When people are trained to perform such activities, they generally start out by memorizing what it is they have to do (see if you can remember what should be done if you see smoke coming from an oven). This type of knowledge is termed *declarative knowledge* because it consists of declarative statements, for example a fire extinguisher is used to put out fires. The important point to grasp is that declarative knowledge is at the level of *verbal knowledge*, that is, the kind of knowledge you get from books, instructions, or being told what to do.

In order to achieve skilled performance you need to be able to translate declarative knowledge into actions, known as *procedural knowledge*. A good example is learning to drive a car: there is the world of difference between knowing how to change gears, and being able to do it. In the initial stages of learning from instructions people often forget one or another of the components. With practice, skilled performance becomes better integrated, and speeds up considerably. In other words, the expert learns to respond to whole patterns rather than to individual components of a situation. (The driver 'changes down to third' instead of 'moving the gear lever from the bottom right position to the top right'.)

In ACT, Anderson claims that people progress through three successive stages of learning in acquiring cognitive skills.

1 The first stage of learning involves the accumulation of domain relevant facts which are incorporated into the system's declarative network structure. In learning chess, for example, a novice would acquire a number of facts or rules governing the direction of moves possible for each chess piece, such as: 'a bishop can be moved along diagonals' or 'a knight can be moved forward (sideways, backward) two squares and over one square'. Pre-existing general problem-solving processes (for example, working backwards) would then employ these facts in solving problems. A major advantage of declarative knowledge is that it is general in the sense that there is no commitment to its use in some specific manner, such as would be the case if the knowledge were represented procedurally. The main drawback of declarative knowledge is that before it can be used it must be retrieved and kept active in working memory. In ACT, the slow pace and tentative nature of problem solving during this stage of learning are attributed to the need to activate and retrieve declarative knowledge from long-term memory, for example, rules about the direction in which a knight may be moved. Also, loss of information from working memory is seen as a major source of errors during problem solving.

2 With experience, however, Anderson claims that declarative knowledge becomes proceduralized. In this second, *transitional stage* of learning, to use the terminology of production systems, new productions are created from the declarative knowledge acquired during the first stage of learning. The mechanism underlying the transition between the first two stages is called *proceduralization*. Proceduralization is a mechanism that transforms declarative information in long-term memory into procedures for actions. The outcome of proceduralization is that declarative knowledge becomes embedded in procedures, and the result of the process is that memory

retrieval becomes unnecessary. Elimination of the retrieval of information not only has the effect of speeding up performance but also reduces the load on working memory. The operation of the proceduralization mechanism will be further elaborated in Section 4.4.

3 In the final stage of learning in ACT, the *procedural stage*, the productions that have been acquired are *tuned*, or smoothed out. In essence, during this stage the learner acquires considerable knowledge about the conditions in which a production should fire. In this stage the learner also generalizes what has been learned, and the application of knowledge speeds up considerably. In ACT, speed-up in performance is partly attributed to a mechanism called *composition*. The operation of the composition mechanism is described in Section 4.3 and an example of generalization in Section 4.5.

4.2 A production system model of column addition

The behaviour of the ACT system will be illustrated with respect to a simple addition problem. This will give us an opportunity to look in detail at a production system that contains many of the component processes of a particular skill. Although the production system has only twelve rules, you will be able to see for yourself the complexities involved in modelling a process which most people would consider fairly 'obvious' or 'easy'.

Imagine that we have set out to construct a computer model of the way a child performs column addition. As a first step, consider that we arranged to videotape a young girl while she performed a long series of column addition exercises, such as the one given in Figure 3.4. We have decided to call our computer model ADDY, so throughout the discussion we will refer to our little subject as Addy too.

$$\begin{array}{ccc}
3 & 5 & 6 \\
1 & 3 & 2 \\
8 & 2 & 4 \\
\hline
\end{array}$$

Figure 3.4   Answer:

Our immediate goal is to create a production system model of Addy's performance (we can worry about modelling learning in later sections). This involves trying to identify the component processes of addition and then writing production rules that reflect the operation of each of these components. The first step is to try to uncover the conditions that trigger particular actions when Addy does addition problems.

125

When we sit down together to replay the videotapes we find that during the first few sessions Addy always follows the same routine in doing addition problems: she always starts with the number in the top row of the righthand column, says the number out loud, puts a tick next to the number with her pencil to indicate that it has been counted, and moves down one row to the next number, adds it to the running total, ticks it, and so on. When she finishes adding the numbers in the righthand column, Addy writes down the answer if it is less than ten and moves over to the number in the top row of the middle column and follows the same routine as before. If the product of one column of numbers is equal to or greater than ten, then Addy writes the second digit of the product under the column, and carries the first digit over to the next column, where she adds it to the number in the top row. If there is a 'carry' after Addy has processed the final column, she writes the second digit of the answer under the column and then writes the first digit of the answer to the immediate left.

The following figure highlights some of the conditions (that is, the IF parts of production rules that we want to construct) for Addy's different actions (which are the THEN parts of the rules).

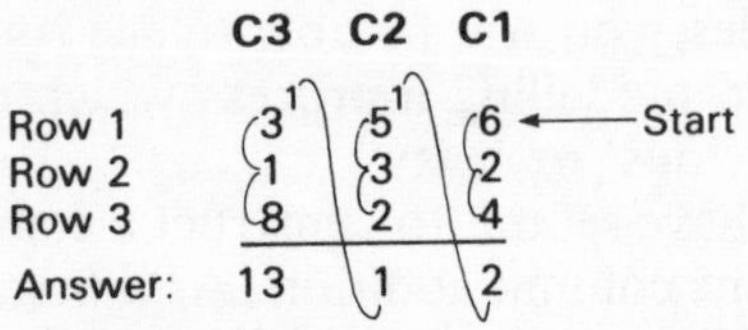

Figure 3.5

In Figure 3.5 the addition problem is represented as a problem involving the iterative, or cyclic, processing of the columns, starting with the righthand column (labelled C1 for column 1 in Figure 3.5), and then iterating leftward through any remaining columns (for example, columns C2 and C3, respectively, in three-column addition problems). Within any given column the solving process involves iterating through all the rows of the column. A third main process, not shown in Figure 3.5 but inferred from Addy's verbal behaviour during the task, is the retrieval of number facts from long-term memory during each iteration through the rows of a column.

A distinctive feature of the performance is its hierarchical goal/sub-goal structure. The highest level goal is to do a series of addition problems. This goal is broken down into the goals of doing the first problem in a set, and of then doing the rest of the problems. The goal of doing a single problem is broken down into the sub-goal of iterating through the columns of the problem, and within this sub-goal there is the sub-goal of iterating through the rows of each column.

Our next step is to express these aspects of Addy's performance in a set of production rules. Table 3.1 contains a set of rules (adapted from Anderson, 1982) that in fact captures a lot of the detail of the component processes. In Table 3.1 Addy's performance is presented as three main groups of productions – P1-P5, P6-P9 and P10-P12 – each group reflecting a set of related processes.

Productions P1 to P5 encapsulate Addy's knowledge about iterating through the columns of an addition problem.

Production P1 states that, if Addy has the goal of doing an addition problem, she should have the sub-goal of iterating through all of the columns of the problem.

P2 states that if Addy has the sub-goal of iterating through the columns of a problem, she should first of all process the righthand column by iterating through the rows of that column. P2 also states that the running total should be set to 0 at the start of a new problem. (Imagine what would happen if a child forgot to eliminate the sum of a previous problem when a new problem was begun.)

P3 would apply whenever Addy has finished with a column and there is another column to the left. This rule is general enough to ensure that all columns would get processed no matter how many columns of figures are given in a particular problem.

P4 and P5 both contain the 'stopping rule' for an addition problem. In effect, the rules say that, if there are no more columns to be

Table 3.1

P1	IF	the current goal is to do an addition problem
	THEN	the sub-goal is to iterate through the columns of the problem
P2	IF	the current goal is to iterate through the columns of an addition problem
	THEN	the sub-goal is to iterate through the rows of column 1 and set the running total to 0
P3	IF	the current goal is to iterate through the columns of an addition problem and a column has just been processed and there is another column to the left of the previous column
	THEN	the sub-goal is to iterate through the rows of the next column
P4	IF	the current goal is to iterate through the columns of an addition problem and a column has just been processed and there is no column to the left of the previous column and the running total is total
	THEN	write out total in the answer space at the bottom of the column and mark the goal as achieved

P5   IF the current goal is to iterate through the columns of an addition problem
and a column has just been processed
and there is no column to the left of the previous column
and the running total is 0
THEN mark the goal as achieved

P6   IF the current goal is to iterate through the rows of a column
and the top row has not been processed
THEN the sub-goal is to add the number of the top row into the running total

P7   IF the current goal is to iterate through the rows of a column
and a row has just been processed
and another lower row is below this row
THEN the sub-goal is to add the number of the lower row into the running total

P8   IF the current goal is to iterate through the rows of a column
and a row has just been processed
and there is not another row below this row
and the running total is total
and total is a digit
THEN write the total in the answer space at the bottom of the column
and the running total is 0
and mark the column as processed
and mark the goal as achieved

P9   IF the current goal is to iterate through the rows of a column
and a row has just been processed
and there is not another row below this row
and the running total is total
and total is of the form digit 1 and then digit 2
THEN write digit 2 in the answer space at the bottom of the column
and the running total is digit 1
and mark the column as processed
and mark the goal as achieved

P10   IF the current goal is to add number 1 to number 2
and number 2 is a digit
and number 1 + number 2 = sum
THEN make the new running total as the sum
and mark the number 1 as processed
and mark the goal as achieved

P11   IF the current goal is to add number 1 to number 2
and number 2 is of the form digit 1 and then digit 2
and number 1 + digit 2 = sum
and sum is less than 10

THEN   make the new running total digit 1 followed by sum
and mark the number 1 as processed
and mark the goal as achieved

P12   IF   the current goal is to add number 1 to number 2
and number 2 is of the form digit 1 and then digit 2
and number 1 + digit 2 = sum
and sum is of the form 1 and digit 3
and 1 + digit 1 = units-sum

THEN   the new running total is units-sum and then digit 3
and mark the number as processed
and mark the goal as achieved

---

processed then Addy should write out the answer and stop. P4 and P5 differ in their specification of the way an answer should be written, dependent upon whether the answer is less than ten or is equal to or greater than ten.

Productions P6 to P9 reflect Addy's knowledge about processing the rows of an addition problem.

P6 would direct Addy to start at the top row when she first starts processing any column, and to add the value of the first digit into the running total (the carry), whatever that happens to be.

P7 directs Addy to the next row in a column, and contains an instruction to add the next number to the running total.

P8 contains information about what to do when there are no more rows in a particular column, and the running total is a single digit (a number less than 10). The rule states that the carry should be set to 0, and that the column should be marked as having been processed. This last instruction will help Addy to decide what to do on the next cycle. The rule also contains an instruction to note that the current goal has now been achieved.

P9 is like P8 but is applicable whenever the result is a two-digit number, such as '28'. In this case, the instructions are to write the second digit (8) in the answer space for the current column, and to make the first digit (2) the carry, by making that the new value of the running total.

Addy's knowledge about adding numbers together is contained in productions P10 to P12. These productions retrieve number addition facts from long-term memory.

There are a number of ways in which these rules are quite 'magical'. For instance, some of the information required at any step in the problem would be stored in working memory (for example, the current running total), and other information would be present either in the problem itself (the actual numbers in a column) or in

129

long-term memory (number addition facts, knowledge about whether a number is a single digit). We have not addressed issues about how problem information is brought into working memory by the operation of perceptual processes, or how information is retrieved from working memory. A complete model of column addition would have to deal with these problems.

Note also that this production system involves matching rules to the same data elements (goals) on successive cycles. This would seem to be a contradiction of our earlier discussion of the 'refractoriness' conflict resolution rule (see Section 3.2), which disallowed such an operation. But remember also that in Section 3 we discussed production systems as general frameworks for cognitive modelling, and pointed out that individual modellers adapt the framework to suit their own purposes. In the ADDY production system, we are using goals to keep the system focused on a single goal, such as iterating through the rows of a column, throughout the addition task. Production selection would be restricted to productions that are related to the current (latest) goal in working memory. When the current goal has been achieved, it would be 'removed' from working memory, and the next most recent goal would then be the focus of the system's attention.

4.3 Learning: composition of productions

In the previous section we presented a model of Addy's performance during her first few sessions doing addition problems. Now we want to consider her performance towards the end of the experiment. As before, we sit down together to analyse the videotapes of the final sessions, and we find a number of differences between her earlier performance and the way she deals with addition problems now. The most prominent difference is that Addy now solves each problem about five times as fast as she did at the start of the experiment. Also, Addy no longer talks aloud while she is working on the problems and has stopped putting ticks on the problem sheets as she adds the numbers together. In short, practice has had the result of making Addy a lot more efficient and faster at doing column addition problems; in fact, she has become an expert.

The question that we will now address concerns the mechanisms underlying her learning processes. In this section I will describe composition, a process that transforms small components of a skill into 'macro' components, or macro-operators. In composition, *a new production is constructed from a pair of already existing productions* which are related to the same goal, and which occur reliably in succession during problem solving.

The composition process creates a new production by putting together all of the clauses in the IF part of the first production with all of the clauses in the IF part of the second production *except any clauses that also appear in the THEN part of the first production.* The THEN part of the new production would contain all of the THEN clauses of both productions.

The composition formula can be expressed in the following terms:

> The IF side of a new production should contain $A + (C - B)$ and the THEN side should contain $B + D$ of the productions being composed, where A = the IF part of the first production, B = the THEN part of the first production, C = the IF part of the second production, and D = the THEN part of the second production.

In order to see how this formula is used to compose two productions together, consider productions P1 and P2 from the ADDY production system, with their parts labelled according to the composition formula.

P1   (A)   IF the goal is to do an addition problem

    (B)   THEN the sub-goal is to iterate through the columns of the problem

P2   (C)   IF the sub-goal is to iterate through the columns of an addition problem
and the righthand column has not been processed

    (D)   THEN the sub-goal is to iterate through the rows of the righthand column
and set the running total to 0

Here, the IF clause of P1 corresponds to the A term in the composition formula and the THEN clause corresponds to the B term. The IF clauses of P2 correspond to the C term of the formula, and the THEN clauses correspond to the D term. Now, according to the formula, a new production, P3, could be formed by creating an IF part containing the clauses in A (the goal is to do an addition problem) *plus* all of the clauses in C (the goal is to iterate through the columns of an addition problem, and the righthand column has not been processed) except those that also occur in B (the sub-goal is to iterate through the columns of an addition problem).

Creating the THEN side of the new production simply involves putting together the B and D clauses (that is, the THEN clauses of both productions). When this happens, the whole of the new production looks like the formula overleaf:

P1   IF the goal is to do an addition problem
           and the righthand column has not been processed

    THEN the sub-goal is to iterate through the columns of the
         problem
         and within this the sub-goal is to iterate through the
         rows of the righthand column
         and set the running total to 0

SAQ 20
The following pair of productions for dialling the first two digits of a telephone
number would always be activated in succession. Using the composition mechanism
described on page 131, can you create a new production that does the work of both?
(*Note* Composition also involves deleting redundant clauses. For example, when
the IF parts of two productions contain the same goal clause, the clause should
occur only once in the new, composed production.)

P1   IF the goal is to dial a telephone number
           and number 1 is the first digit of the telephone number
    THEN dial number 1

P2   IF the goal is to dial a telephone number
           and number 1 has been dialled
           and number 2 is after number 1 in the telephone number
    THEN dial number 2

Hint The IF part of the new production (which we will again call P3 for the sake
of convenience) would have three clauses and the THEN part would have two
clauses:

P3   IF (condition 1)
           and (condition 2)
           and (condition 3)

    THEN (action 1)
         (action 2)

As learning proceeds, composition would allow more and more components of a performance to be integrated. The composed productions would contain complex conditional patterns that would serve
as the conditions for the performance of an equally complex, but
well practised, sequence of actions. As such, the composition process
helps to explain some aspects of the transition from novice to expert
performance.

4.4   Proceduralization and strengthening

Another automatic learning process described by Anderson, and
utilized in the ACT system, involves transforming declarative
knowledge into procedural form in the way that was outlined briefly
in Section 4.1. Again the process involves the construction of new
productions, but in proceduralization the process involves creating

new productions that directly encode the problem information and information which is retrieved from long-term memory during problem solving.

In order to see what is involved in proceduralization, consider the following 'number addition' production which a child might possess.

> IF the goal is to add number 1 to number 2
> and number 1 + number 2 = number 3
> THEN say number 3

The first conditional clause of the production would match information in a problem, for example, the problem of adding five and six together. Assume that a child has memorized some number addition facts. Such facts would be stored as declarative knowledge in long-term memory, and would be retrieved as a result of a match between this knowledge and the second conditional clause of the number addition production.

In ACT, whenever a situation arises in which a production uses problem information and declarative information retrieved from long-term memory, a new production containing both types of information is constructed.

In the example, proceduralization would create a production of the form

> IF the goal is to add 5 to 6
> THEN say 11

so that in future the goal of adding five to six would be achieved directly, without the need to retrieve the information from the declarative network in long-term memory.

ACT also employs a *strengthening* mechanism which operates on both declarative knowledge and production rules. New productions are added to production memory with a strength equal to one. Each time the production is used, its strength is incremented by one. Productions that are used frequently thus become quite strong. Productions that are infrequently or never used after they have been created are weakened over time because of a decrement process built into ACT. Children tend to be given regular addition exercises and are thus offered repeated opportunities to apply the same addition rules over and over again. ACT's proceduralization and strengthening processes, together with the composition process described in the previous section, suggest types of mechanisms that could explain the speed up in performance which results from such practice, and forms part of the learning process.

4.5   Generalization

In his descriptions of ACT, Anderson provides a number of examples of *generalization* in problem solving, but these are too
complex to discuss here. Instead, I will describe a simple example of
generalization in language acquisition. The generalization process
involves making alterations to the conditions of a production so that
the same action can be applied in a wide range of new but similar circumstances. For instance, consider the following two productions
(from Anderson, 1983);

P1   IF the goal is to indicate that a coat belongs to me

    THEN say 'My coat'

P2   IF the goal is to indicate that a ball belongs to me

    THEN say 'My ball'

The only difference between these two productions is the object that
is referred to, 'coat' and 'ball' respectively. ACT has mechanisms for
discovering a pair of productions that have a lot in common, and a
number of mechanisms for making the productions more general. In
a case such as this, a more general production could be created by
constructing a rule that contained a *variable* in place of the specific
objects mentioned in the original productions.

In a production system, or any other programming system, a
variable is a special symbol that can stand for different things during
different applications of the program. All that is required is that the
pattern matcher should be designed to treat variables in a special way
whenever they are encountered. One way to do this would be to
design a pattern matcher that allows any symbol in a production rule
that is prefixed by, say, a question mark, to match anything in a
working-memory pattern that occurs in the same place in both the
rule and the pattern. Also, as soon as a variable takes on a 'value'
in pattern matching, all other occurrences of the same variable in the
same production take on the same value.

The following production (P1*) is a generalized version of productions P1 and P2:

P1*   IF the goal is to indicate that a certain object belongs to
    me

    THEN say 'My (object)'

How might this generalization process work to explain responses to
new situations? Suppose the language learner's working memory
contains the following pattern,

    my goal is to indicate that the tricycle belongs to me

Since there is no specific production rule to deal with this, a match will be found between this pattern and the conditional clause of the general production rule about possession of objects. As a result the (object) variable in P1* would be filled by 'tricycle', triggering the response 'My tricycle'.

Basically, the generalization process is a mechanism for finding *analogies* between the present situation and other earlier learnt conditions, and creating a production that captures these similarities. The importance of exploiting analogies between similar problems was stressed in Part II, where we discussed research in which Gick and Holyoak, and Reed, Ettinger and Dempster attempted to teach people generalized problem-solving schemas for detecting analogies. The generalization mechanisms incorporated in ACT help us to understand the complexity of the processes involved in generalizing the solutions of similar problems.

4.6   Evaluation of the ACT learning theory

Anderson and his various collaborators have constructed a number of computer programs to test the assumptions embodied in ACT and have compared the performance of the programs with human performance in a number of different learning environments. Examples are computer programming (Anderson, Farrell and Sauers, 1984; Pirolli and Anderson, 1985), geometry (Anderson, Greeno, Kline and Neves, 1981) and language acquisition (Anderson, 1983).

The models provide quite detailed accounts of problem solving and learning in all of the domains that have been studied. In particular, they show how a learning system which starts off with only a number of domain related facts stored in declarative long-term memory, plus a number of pre-existing general problem-solving procedures (such as procedures for working through a list of problems, and for solving problems by analogy to worked out examples presented in instructional material), can acquire new procedures that are responsive to the kind of situations that occur in the domain of learning. The simulations demonstrate that skill acquisition can be modelled by the addition and modification of production rules. Mechanisms such as proceduralization and composition transform a system that initially works backwards (novice strategy) into one that works forwards (like experts).

The main problem with the simulations is that they often perform better than the human subjects whose behaviour they are meant to model. As an example, Anderson (1982) describes a simulation of the behaviour of high-school students solving two-column proof problems in geometry. The 'simulation' solved these problems but not all the students did. In fact, simulations based on ACT often seem to provide us with models of the idealized problem solving and learning of 'good' students, rather than of the average student who experiences considerable difficulty in solving problems and learning to derive procedures from declarative instructions.

Summary of Section 4

- ACT models learning in terms of adding and altering productions in long-term production memory.
- In ACT, knowledge is represented in both declarative and procedural form. In the initial stage of skill acquisition, knowledge is represented as a number of facts in propositional network structures in long-term memory. The second stage of learning involves the transformation of declarative knowledge into procedures for applying knowledge directly. During the final stage of learning, procedural knowledge is refined by processes such as composition, generalization and strengthening.
- Composition is a process that constructs 'macro-operators' by combining a pair of productions that are related to the same goal, and that reliably follow one another in a problem-solving task.
- The generalization process makes alterations to the condition part of similar productions so that the production can apply in other similar, but novel conditions.
- Production rules are strengthened with use. New productions enter the system with a strength equal to 1. Each time a production rule is applied its strength is automatically increased. Production rules that apply infrequently gradually lose strength through an automatic strength decrement process.

Overview

In this overview I would like to draw out some of the main implications of the research discussed in the book. I will confine my discussion to the implications of research on learning on the basis of analogical problem solving and search in problem spaces, and individual differences in problem solving.

Analogical problem solving and learning

The book began with a review of research on human problem solving on a number of very simple, puzzle-like transformation problems such as the Towers of Hanoi. The research on transfer of learning discussed in Part I revealed that people may experience considerable difficulty in transferring what they know about solving a problem of a particular type when they are confronted with a new problem of the same type. This research showed that subjects sometimes had to be told the relationship between two problems before they could apply previously acquired knowledge in solving a new problem, and even then previous experience was no help if the new problem was more complex than the earlier one.

Another way of conceptualizing the problem of transfer between problems is to ask whether people can see the analogies between similar problems and can exploit these to solve novel problems.

In Part II we found conflicting evidence about people's ability to exploit analogies between similar problems. On the one hand, Gick and Holyoak's research on the radiation problem indicates that people are unlikely to use a prior analogy (the fortress problem) unless they are given a hint to do so. Nevertheless, they are quite successful at using analogies once the idea has been suggested to them. On the other hand, the results of experiments conducted by Reed, Dempster and Ettinger on students' ability to use worked-out solutions of algebra problems suggest that people may experience considerable difficulty in applying analogies in more realistic, classroom situations. Taken together, the findings indicate that people are rather poor at transferring knowledge from one situation to another without considerable guidance. This conclusion is supported by the results of research reported in Part II in which it was shown that experimental subjects were unlikely to construct an abstract schema for similar problems unless they were presented with at least a couple of closely related problems, and provided with information on the principle that united them.

All this has considerable implications for learning, since most teaching is based on the notion that students can learn to extract general principles from problem-solving experiences which they can apply to solve other similar problems.

So, what can we learn from problem-solving research about how to design teaching materials? Textbooks on subjects such as mathematics, physics or computer programming usually contain a number of main sections in which principles are defined and discussed. Principles are sometimes illustrated with a worked-out example. Students are then presented with a number of practice problems which are designed to provide the student with the know-how to apply the principles to all problems of that type.

Research into analogical problem solving, though, suggests that the relationship between the original worked-out example and the exercise problems should not be left to students to puzzle out for themselves, but should be made explicit. Although this might seem just plain common sense, the fact is that many textbook writers do not employ such principles. For example, I know of one standard textbook on computer programming in which exercise problems bear only the most tenuous relationship with the worked-out examples used for teaching purposes in earlier parts of the text.

Search in problem spaces

In Part I the notion of state space analysis was introduced. This is a method for setting out all possible moves allowed by the rules of a problem. Finding the solution to a problem can be defined as discovering an appropriate path through the possible moves. Such an objective analysis of the overall structure of a problem is only possible for puzzles with a limited number of set moves which can be defined beforehand. For most real-life problems it would be impossible to list a set of predefined possible moves. Moreover, even with puzzle problems, novices are unlikely to appreciate the overall structure of the problem. Simon and Polson's models, introduced in Part I, are both concerned with the *mental* problem spaces which are extracted from people's personal understanding of a problem; and also with the limitations on problem solving as a result of short-term memory limitations.

According to the information processing model, people proceed in solving such problems by making local decisions, based on means-ends analysis. People are unable to plan a sequence of moves even on transformation puzzle problems, for example, the Waterjugs problem, because they begin with a very limited understanding of the structure of the problem and because working memory capacity is insufficient to hold all the move information necessary for forward planning. People often get lost in such problems because the means-ends strategy of evaluating distance from the goal leads them away from the solution at certain critical points in the problem. According to Polson, subjects get themselves out of trouble on this task simply by learning to avoid moves that take them back to previously visited states in the problem. On the face of it, this might seem to be a very weak heuristic for guiding search for a solution to a problem.

Anzai and Simon (Part III, Section 3) also demonstrated how relatively weak strategies, such as avoiding return to previous states of a problem, could be very useful in understanding and solving problems for which no guidance is provided. In essence, they show how initial attempts at solving the Towers of Hanoi problem could be viewed as a kind of 'exploration' of the problem space. During this exploration, a solver might learn to identify moves that lead to dead-ends, and so to avoid such moves on subsequent attempts at the problem. Avoiding bad moves considerably reduces the size of the problem space. The effect of a reduced problem space would be to make it more likely that a solver will see what leads to what on paths near to the optimal solution path of a problem. Discovering what leads to what makes it more likely that solvers will be able to identify useful sub-goals in solving a problem. If a solver can devise a plan for achieving sub-goals on the next attempt, the problem space might be even further reduced. In other words, initial attempts at solving a problem may set up the conditions for applying more powerful heuristics, such as means-ends analysis, on subsequent attempts at the problem.

The analysis is interesting because we can see how it relates to problem solving and learning in more realistic task environments. If you watch novice students trying to solve problems in domains such as computer programming or mathematics, you will often see them selecting operators almost at random. The student may make ten attempts at solving a problem, 'getting nowhere fast'. But with enough persistence, the student may find a solution, perhaps without understanding it, simply by a process of elimination of operators that led nowhere on previous attempts at the problem. As Simon points out, having a solution to a problem, even a solution that is achieved without understanding while the problem is being solved, provides a basis for further learning. In the Towers of Hanoi problem, knowing the solution to the problem provided the subject with a 'worked-out example' of how the problem could be solved. The worked-out example then served as a basis for further understanding of the problem. In order to see how this process of learning from worked-out examples might occur in learning in more complex domains, we shall now turn to an examination of the role of means-ends analysis in learning from examples.

Novices and experts

In Part III we discussed research on learning in a variety of domains, such as computer programming, physics and mathematics. These were described as semantically rich, formal domains. We saw that in every case experts differed from novices not only in the amount of domain specific knowledge they acquired, but also in the way their knowledge was organized and used. We also discussed production systems as formalisms for representing knowledge and skills. Anzai and Simon showed how learning could be modelled as the addition of new production rules and by the adaptation of rules already existing in production memory. We also discussed ACT, the cognitive learning theory developed by John Anderson, which attempts to explain procedural learning as the *proceduralization* of declarative knowledge through practice at solving problems. ACT also contains mechanisms such as *composition*, *strengthening*, and *generalization* for combining and tuning the production rules that are acquired through proceduralization.

At the present time, most students learn how to solve domain related problems efficiently only by devoting hundreds or thousands of hours of their time to solving such problems. Unfortunately, it is often only the 'better' students who benefit from such practice. However, an important 'spin off' of research on novice/expert differences has been the identification of many of the strategies experts use in solving problems in particular domains, and psychologists have begun to explore the possibility that novices might be taught domain specific problem-solving strategies directly.

This possibility has been explored by Schoenfeld (1979), whose research suggests that students can indeed be taught useful problem-solving strategies. Schoenfeld used two groups of students who spent twenty hours solving mathematics problems. Both groups performed about equally well on a pre-experimental test that involved solving a small number of mathematics problems. An experimental group was then presented with a list of useful problem-solving strategies and were given practice at applying the strategies on twenty exercise problems. The control group was also asked to solve the exercise problems, but was not given instruction in the use of special strategies. In a post-experimental test, the experimental subjects were able to solve approximately three times as many problems as they had solved in the pre-experimental test. The control subjects showed no improvement at all on the post-experimental problems.

We began this book with a discussion of human problem solving on relatively simple puzzle problems and ended with a description of computer models of the problem solving and learning processes that occur when people learn complex, specialized topics such as mathematics. Cognitive psychologists have made considerable contributions to our understanding of problem solving and learning over the past two decades, and all the signs point to further increases in that understanding in the future.

Answers to SAQs

SAQ 1

A minimum of seven moves is necessary for solving the three-ring version of the Towers of Hanoi problem. The moves involved in moving three rings from Peg A to Peg B are:

> small ring from Peg A to Peg B;
>
> medium ring from Peg A to Peg C;
>
> small ring from Peg B to Peg C;
>
> large ring from Peg A to Peg B;
>
> small ring from Peg C to Peg A;
>
> medium ring from Peg C to Peg B;
>
> small ring from Peg A to Peg B.

SAQ 2

(a) Solving a crossword puzzle clue.
   Initial state: a string of empty squares.
   Goal state: the squares filled in with the words indicated by the crossword clues.
(b) Playing noughts and crosses.
   Initial state: a three-by-three matrix of empty cells.
   Goal state: a winning line of noughts or crosses.

SAQ 3

The text points out that the degree to which a problem is considered ill or well defined often depends upon the solver's knowledge. People who have done a lot of travelling will have acquired knowledge about appropriate travelling operators and the situations in which they apply. For such people, most travel problems would be pretty well defined. The less experience a person has with such problems, the more likely that the problem will seem ill defined.

SAQ 4

(a) From state 3 the graph can be extended by moving the medium-sized ring from Peg A to Peg C.

(b) From state 3 it is possible to reach state 1 (a loop), state 2 and state 5, as indicated by the lines emanating from state 3.

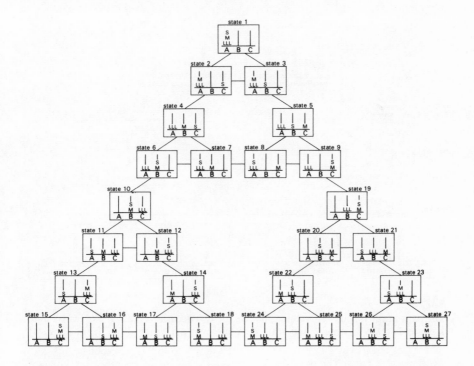

SAQ 5

Initial state: Three people, a Host, a Senior Guest, and a Junior Guest. The Host performs three services for his guests. Each task has a different degree of nobility associated with it. The tasks are stoking the fire (least noble), pouring the tea (medium nobility), and reciting poetry (most noble).

Goal state: The Senior Guest performs all three services for the Host and Junior Guest.

Operators: Host and guests can ask to perform a task currently being perfomed by any of the others.

Operator restrictions: No one can ask to perform a task which is nobler than any task(s) currently being performed. Only one task may be requested at a time.

SAQ 6

Since the three-task Chinese Tea Ceremony problem and the three-ring Towers of Hanoi problem are completely isomorphic (have the same state space) they can both be solved in seven moves.

Answers to SAQs

SAQ 7

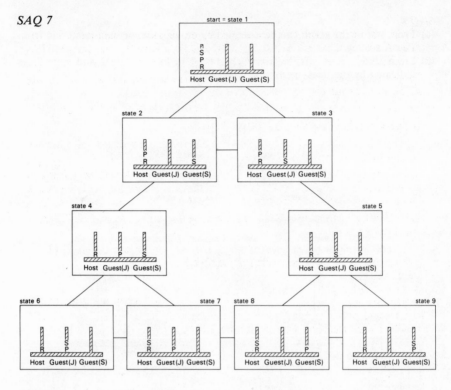

SAQ 8

The path I take through this state space on the few occasions that I make tea is: state 1, state 2, state 5, state 7 and state 8. Your own path may differ from mine, of course.

SAQ 9

(a) There are two paths through the state space for the 8, 5, 3 Waterjugs problem; one path involves seven moves, the other eight moves.
(b) I don't know how may steps you needed to solve the problem, but from experience of watching others solve it, I'd say it took considerably more than seven or eight.
(c) Many people complain that they don't see what they should be doing in solving this problem. Even when people set up intermediate sub-goals, such as getting one litre of water into the 5-litre jug and three litres of water into the 3-litre jug, they find that they are unable to plan a sequence of moves that would get them to such a state.

SAQ 10

(a) At line 1 of the protocol (see below) the subject seems to be making an evaluation of her own progress on the problem, so I labelled the line META-COMMENT.

I labelled line 2 REHEARSAL because it appears that the subject is refreshing her memory about the current state of the problem.

The statement in line 3 seems to reflect a MOVE GENERATION process.

At line 4, another MOVE GENERATION.

At line 5 the subject seems to be evaluating the possible moves generated in lines 3 and 4 of the protocol, so I labelled the line as EVALUATION.

The statement in line 6 reflects a decision about the move the subject intends to make. Further evidence for this is the fact that the subject immediately made the move. I thought this reflected a MOVE SELECTION process.

I labelled line 7 MEMORY UPDATE because the subject, having just made a move, describes the new current state of the problem.

1 I'm not getting very far with this.	META-COMMENT
2 The five-litre jug and the three-litre jug are both full...	REHEARSAL
3 so I can either pour the three litres into the eight-litre jug...	MOVE GENERATION
4 or I could pour the five litres into the eight.	MOVE GENERATION
5 Well, I want the three-litre jug empty, don't I?	EVALUATION
6 So, I want to pour out the three litres into the eight-litre jug.	MOVE SELECTION
7 That means I've got three litres in the eight-litre jug, and five litres in the five-litre jug.	MEMORY UPDATE

(b) The means-ends value for the first move (in which the subject poured three litres from the eight-litre jug into the three-litre jug) is five, since the resulting state leaves the subject one litre of water away from the goal contents of the eight-litre jug and four litres away from the goal contents of the five-litre jug.

The means-ends value for the second move is also five, since the resulting state (0, 5, 3) now reverses the previous situation. Here the subject needs four litres of water in the eight-litre jug, and must get rid of one litre of water in the five-litre jug in order to attain the goal.

The means-ends value for the third move drops to two, since the subject has reached a state in which she has one litre of water too little in the eight-litre jug and one litre too much in the five-litre jug.

You can check these values by referring to the state space graph in Figure 1.14.

Answers to SAQs

SAQ 11

Initial state: General outside fortress with army. Tyrant inside fortress. Roads radiating out from the fortress have been mined. Large bodies of men passing along a road would set off mines, destroying the roads and making them impassable. If the roads are destroyed the tyrant would destroy many villages in retaliation.

Goal: General overthrows tyrant.

Operators: General can use army to attack fortress.

Operator restrictions: General must avoid destruction of army and villages.

SAQ 12

The fortress problem is ill defined because the operator ('use army') is underspecified. The general's problem is to determine more precisely how the army can be used to achieve the goal, without violating the operator restrictions. The problem is solved when the general transforms the general operator 'use army' into specific actions that can be performed, such as 'divide army', 'send small units along roads', and so on.

SAQ 13

Initial state: Tumour in patient's stomach. Doctor is not allowed to operate. Doctor has special ray which can be used for treatment. High intensity rays destroy healthy tissue as well as tumours. Low intensity rays neither destroy tumours nor damage healthy tissue.

Goal: Doctor destroys tumour.

Operators: Doctor can use special rays to destroy tumour.

Operator restrictions: Doctor must avoid damage to healthy tissue.

SAQ 14

The radiation problem is ill defined because the operator ('use rays') is underspecified. The doctor's problem is to determine more precisely how the rays can be used to achieve the goal, without violating the operator restrictions. The problem is solved when the doctor transforms the general operator 'use rays' into specific actions that can be performed, such as 'send several low intensity rays from many different directions simultaneously towards site of tumour'.

SAQ 15

In Gick and Holyoak's research subjects who were given a hint that there was a relationship between the radiation problem and the fortress problem performed better than subjects who were not given such a hint. Subjects were also able to use a very general hint about the relationship between the radiation problem and the fortress problem as shown by the results of the experiment in which the fortress problem story was presented along with two other problem stories that were disanalogous to the radiation problem. In this situation, subjects who were given the general hint produced dispersion solutions to the radiation problem significantly more frequently than subjects who were not given a hint. These findings suggest that inability to notice spontaneously an analogy is the major impediment to analogical problem solving; that applying a known solution in a new problem situation is not a major stumbling block.

However, in the research reported by Reed *et al.*, subjects found a hint about the relationship between closely related problems useful only if the second problem was somewhat less complex (measured in terms of the number of possible illegal problem states) than the first problem. This finding suggests that solution processes are as important as noticing processes in analogical problem solving.

Gick and Holyoak point out that the problems used by Reed *et al.* are computational, or multistep problems, and that the solutions to such problems may be difficult to remember. It is also possible that multistep solutions are simply too difficult to apply to new problems because of processing limitations such as limited working-memory capacity.

SAQ 16

(a) I would call the common causal relation something like 'avoidance', since Debbie's goal seems to be to avoid John, and George's goal seems to be to avoid the police.

(b) On a similarity scale of 1 to 10, I would say that on the surface the stories should be given a score of 1. If the scale had been 0 to 10, I would have rated them as having zero similarity on the surface, since in the one case we are dealing with a story about a conversation between two women, one of whom later moved out of town, and in the other case a story about a man who seems to decide not to return home while a police car sits in front of his house.

(c) I would give these stories a similarity rating of about 10 on the basis of the causal relation identified in (a). However, if I took other factors into consideration (such as the motives I would attribute to either Debbie or George in wanting to avoid an old flame or ex-husband (my inference), on the one hand, or a jail term (another inference) on the other, then I would suggest a lower rating.

SAQ 17

(a) Reassembling a wardrobe looks like a problem of *sequence inversion*, such as rescrewing parts that had been unscrewed when the wardrobe was disassembled.

(b) The problem of telephoning for a seat reservation looks like a problem involving two solution transformation operators. Firstly, telephoning for a reservation is a new first step in the plan, and thus involves *initial segment concatenation*. Secondly, *general deletion* seems to be needed because queuing up in order to purchase a ticket at the cinema is no longer necessary if a reservation has been made, so this step should be dropped from the old plan. However, if a lot of people had the same idea then it might still be necessary to queue up to collect the reserved ticket. A clever planner should be able to look ahead to such possibilities. In such a case it might be better to preserve the queuing step, but with a note indicating circumstances in which the step could be deleted. In this way, the solver could make a decision between two alternatives depending upon the situation that obtains when the plan is being carried out.

(c) Getting somebody else to act as an agent in pursuit of a goal is an instance of the *sub-goal preserving substitution operator*. In this particular case the goal of having a reserved seat is preserved by asking someone else to make the reservation when the solver is prevented from taking direct action.

Answers to SAQs

SAQ 18

My production set for making a cup of tea contains seven production rules. The first production triggers two activities: boiling water and placing a teabag in a cup. The last clause indicates a mental note which serves as one of the setting conditions for P3 (conditional clause 3).

Productions P2a and P2b are responsible for getting a kettle of boiled water. P2a would fire if the kettle was already full of water, and P2b would fire otherwise. P2b's action is simply to fill the kettle with water, which sets up one of the conditions for boiling water in P2a.

P3 would fire whenever (a) the goal was to make a cup of tea, (b) boiling water was available, and (c) there was a cup containing a tea bag (conditions which have been set up by the firing of productions P1 and P2a). The action part of P3 is responsible for filling the cup with boiling water, waiting for the tea to brew, and removing the tea bag.

Productions P4a, P4b and P4c take care of situations where milk and sugar are required, only sugar is required, or only milk is required, respectively. Under the specificity rule of conflict resolution, P4a would fire whenever both sugar and milk were required because it covers more of the conditions of the situation than either P4b or P4c alone. Under the action part of P4 productions the necessary ingredients would be added, the tea stirred, and a note made that the tea was ready for drinking.

Your own production set may look entirely different. If so, don't worry. For one thing, your set may reflect a different ordering of activities. Or you may have performed a much finer-grained analysis of the component processes and, as a result, you may have created a larger number of rules. The important point is the exercise in analysing a behavioural sequence into its component parts and constructing a set of rules that reflect observed behaviour at some level of description.

P1 IF the goal is to make a cup of tea
  THEN boil a kettle of water
    and while the kettle is boiling place a teabag in a cup
    and note that there is a cup containing a teabag

P2a IF the goal is to boil a kettle of water
    and the kettle is full
  THEN plug the kettle into a source of electricity
    and switch the electricity on
    and wait until the water boils
    and note that there is boiling water

P2b IF the goal is to boil a kettle of water
    and the kettle is empty
  THEN fill the kettle with water
    and note that the kettle is full

P3 IF the goal is to make a cup of tea
    and there is boiling water
    and there is a cup containing a teabag
  THEN fill the cup with boiling water
    and wait for one minute for the tea to brew
    and then remove the teabag
    and note that the tea has brewed

P4a IF the goal is to make a cup of tea
    and the tea has brewed
    and sugar and milk are required

THEN add the required amount of sugar
    and then add the milk
    and then stir
    and note that the tea is ready for drinking

P4b   IF the goal is to make a cup of tea
    and the tea has brewed
    and sugar is required
THEN add the required amount of sugar
    and then stir
    and note that the tea is ready for drinking

P4c   IF the goal is to make a cup of tea
    and the tea has brewed
    and milk is required
THEN add the milk
    and then stir
    and note that the tea is ready for drinking

SAQ 19

(a) The loop avoidance strategy would be useful in the Waterjugs problem because it would eliminate any move that was the inverse of the previous move (that is, it would disallow pouring the contents of the five-litre jug into the eight-litre jug as the second move in the problem). The loop avoidance strategy is thus useful in a great number of different situations. In fact, larger looping patterns may occur, as for example when subjects keep returning to an earlier state (the first state on the righthand solution path of the 8, 5, 3 Waterjugs problem, say) from certain states along the solution path (for example, state 6, 2, 0). Polson's subjects had to detect such longer loops through experience, and had to learn to stop making them before they could solve the 8, 5, 3 Waterjugs problem.

(b) The other possible moves, barring a loop, would be to pour from the eight-litre jug into the three-litre jug or to pour from the five-litre jug into the three-litre jug. The first of these moves leads to a 'dead end' (the transition state between the right and left solution paths) and the second move would take the solver forward in the problem.

SAQ 20

Composition of productions P1 and P2 would produce the following production, P3:

P3   IF the goal is to dial a telephone number
    and number 1 is the first digit of the telephone number
    and number 2 is after number 1 in the telephone number
THEN dial number 1
    and then dial number 2

In the composed production, the second clause of P2 ('and number 1 has been dialled') would be deleted because it is essentially the same (except in the details of the wording) as the action in P1 ('dial number 1'). Since the first clause of P1 and P2 is the same ('the goal is to dial a telephone number'), only one instance of the clause would appear in the composed production.

References

ADELSON, B. (1981) 'Problem solving and the development of abstract categories in programming languages', *Memory and Cognition*, 9, pp. 422–33.

AITKENHEAD, A. M. and SLACK, J. M. (1985) *Issues in Cognitive Modeling*, Lawrence Erlbaum Associates (Cognitive Psychology Course Reader).

ANDERSON, J. R. (ed) (1981) *Cognitive Skills and Their Acquisition*, Lawrence Erlbaum Associates.

ANDERSON, J. R. (1982) 'Acquisition of cognitive skill', *Psychological Review*, 89, pp. 369–406.

ANDERSON J. R. (1983) *The Architecture of Cognition*, Harvard University Press.

ANDERSON, J. R., FARRELL, R. and SAUERS, R. (1984) 'Learning to program in LISP', *Cognitive Science*, 8, pp. 87–129.

ANDERSON, J. R., GREENO, J. G., KLINE, P. and NEVES, D. M. (1981) 'Acquisition of problem-solving skill' in J. R. Anderson (1981).

ANZAI, Y. and SIMON, H. A. (1979) 'The theory of learning by doing', *Psychological Review*, 86 (2), pp.124–40.

ATWOOD, M. E., MASSON, M. E. J. and POLSON, P. G. (1980) 'Further explorations with a process model for water jug problems', *Memory and Cognition*, 8 (2), pp. 182–92.

ATWOOD, M. E. and POLSON, P. G. (1976) 'A process model for water jug problems', *Cognitive Psychology*, 8, pp. 191–216.

BHASKAR, R. and SIMON, H. A. (1977) 'Problem solving in semantically rich domains: an example of engineering thermodynamics', *Cognitive Science*, 1, pp. 193–215.

CARBONELL, J. G. (1983) 'Learning by analogy: formulating and generalizing plans from past experience' in R. S. Michalski, J. G. Carbonell and T. M. Mitchell, *Machine Learning: An Artificial Intelligence Approach*, Tioga Publishing Company.

CHASE, W. G. and SIMON, H. A. (1973a) 'Perception in chess', *Cognitive Psychology*, 4, pp. 55–81.

CHASE, W. G. and SIMON, H. A. (1973b) 'The mind's eye in chess' in W. G. Chase (ed) *Visual Information Processing*, Academic Press.

CHI, M. T. H., FELTOVICH, P. J. and GLASER, R. (1981) 'Categorization and representation of physics problems by experts and novices', *Cognitive Science*, 5, pp. 121–52.

COHEN, G., EYSENCK, M. W. and LE VOI, M. E. (1985) *Memory: A Cognitive Approach*, Open University Press (Open Guides to Psychology series).

DE GROOT, A. D. (1965) 'Perception and memory versus thought: some old ideas and recent findings' in B. Kleinmuntz (ed) *Problem Solving*, Riley.

DUNCKER, K. (1945) 'On problem solving', *Psychological Monographs*, 58 (whole no. 270).

ERICSSON, K. A. and SIMON, H. A. (1980) 'Verbal reports as data', *Psychological Review*, 87 (3), pp. 215–51.

ESTES, W. K. (ed) (1978) *Handbook of Learning and Cognitive Processes*, Lawrence Erlbaum Associates.

GENTNER, D. (1979) 'The role of analogical models in learning scientific topics', Technical Report, Bolt, Beranek and Newman.

GENTNER, D. and GENTNER, D. R. (1980) 'Flowing waters or teeming crowds: mental models of electricity' in D. Gentner and A. Stevens (eds) (1983).

GENTNER, D. and STEVENS, A. (eds) (1983) *Mental Models*, Lawrence Erlbaum Associates.

GICK, M. L. and HOLYOAK, K. J. (1980) 'Analogical problem solving', *Cognitive Psychology*, 12, pp. 306–55.

GICK, M. L. and HOLYOAK, K. J. (1983) 'Schema induction and analogical transfer', *Cognitive Psychology*, 15, pp. 1–38.

GREENE, J. and HICKS, C. (1984) *Basic Cognitive Processes*, Open University Press (Open Guides to Psychology series).

GREENO, J. G. (1976) 'Indefinite goals in well-structured problems', *Psychological Review*, 83 (6), pp. 479–91.

GREENO, J. G. (1978) 'Natures of problem-solving abilities' in W. K. Estes (ed) (1978).

HAYES, J. R. (1978) *Cognitive Psychology: Thinking and Creating*, The Dorsey Press.

HAYES, J. R. and SIMON, H. A. (1974) 'Understanding written problem instructions' in L. W. Gregg (ed) *Knowledge and Cognition*, Lawrence Erlbaum Associates.

JEFFRIES, R., POLSON, P. G., RAZRAN, L. and ATWOOD, M. E. (1977) 'A process model for missionaries-cannibals and other river-crossing problems', *Cognitive Psychology*, 9, pp. 412–40.

KINTSCH, W. and VAN DIJK, T. A. (1978) 'Toward a model of text comprehension and production', *Psychological Review*, 85, pp. 363–94.

KOTOVSKY, K., HAYES, J. R. and SIMON, H. A. (1985) 'Why are some problems hard? Evidence from Tower of Hanoi', *Cognitive Science* (in press).

LARKIN, J. H. (1981) 'Enriching formal knowledge: a model for learning to solve textbook physics problems' in J. Anderson (1981).

LUGER, G. F. and BAUER, M. A. (1978) 'Transfer effects in isomorphic problem situations', *Acta Psychologica*.

McKEITHEN, K. B., REITMAN, J. S., RUETER, H. H. and HIRTLE, S. C. (1981) 'Knowledge organization and skill differences in computer programmers', *Cognitive Psychology*, 13, pp. 307–25.

NEWELL, A., SHAW, J. C. and SIMON, H. A. (1958) 'Elements of a theory of human problem solving', *Psychological Review*, 65, pp. 151–66.

NEWELL, A. and SIMON, H. A. (1972) *Human Problem Solving*, Prentice-Hall.

NISBETT, R. E. and WILSON, T. D. (1977) 'Telling more than we can know: verbal reports on mental processes', *Psychological Review*, 84 (3), May, pp. 231–59.

PIROLLI, P. L. and ANDERSON, J. R. (1985) 'The role of learning from examples in the acquisition of recursive programming skills', *Canadian Journal of Psychology* (in press).

POLSON, P. G. and JEFFRIES, R. (1982) 'Problem solving as search and understanding' in R. J. Sternberg (ed) *Advances in the Psychology of Human Intelligence*, Lawrence Erlbaum Associates.

151

References

REED, S. K., DEMPSTER, A. and ETTINGER, M. (1985) 'Usefulness of analogous solutions for solving algebra word problems', *Journal of Experimental Psychology: Learning, Memory and Cognition*, 11 (1), pp. 106–25.

REED, S. K., ERNST, G. W. and BANERJI, R. (1974) 'The role of analogy in transfer between similar problem states', *Cognitive Psychology*, 6, pp. 436–50.

SCHOENFELD, A. H. (1979) 'Explicit heuristic training as a variable in problem-solving performance', *Journal for Research in Mathematics Education*, 10, pp. 173–87.

SIMON, D. P. and SIMON, H. A. (1978) 'Individual differences in solving physics problems' in R. S. Seigler (ed) *Children's Thinking: What Develops?*, Lawrence Erlbaum Associates.

SIMON, H. A. (1978) 'Information processing theories of human problem solving' in W. K. Estes (ed) (1978). Reprinted in A. M. Aitkenhead and J. M. Slack (1985).

SIMON, H. A. and HAYES, J. R. (1976) 'The understanding process: problem isomorphs', *Cognitive Psychology*, 8, pp. 165–90.

THOMAS, J. C. (1974) 'An analysis of behaviour in the hobbits-orcs problem', *Cognitive Psychology*, 6, pp. 257–69.

Index of Authors

Index of concepts

discuss including relev. evidence, the role that
language plays in problem solving.
(piaget)